GWATSON

SEEING AND UNSEEING
SOCIAL STRUCTURE

ABC 6-

SEEING AND UNSEEING SOCIAL STRUCTURE
Sociology's Essential Insights

 **LYNN M. MULKEY**

Hofstra University and
The Board of Education
of the City of New York
Office of Research,
Evaluation, and Assessment

Allyn and Bacon

Boston London Toronto Sydney Tokyo Singapore

Executive Editor: Karen Hanson
Vice-President, Publisher: Susan Badger
Editorial Assistant: Sarah L. Dunbar
Executive Marketing Manager: Joyce Nilsen
Editorial-Production Service: Communicáto, Ltd.
Text Designer: Karen Mason
Manufacturing Buyer: Megan Cochran
Cover Administrator: Linda Knowles
Cover Designer: Suzanne Harbison

Copyright © 1995 by Allyn & Bacon
A Simon & Schuster Company
Needham Heights, Mass. 02194

This book is printed on
recycled, acid-free paper.

Library of Congress Cataloging-in-Publication Data
Mulkey, Lynn Michelle.
    Seeing and unseeing social structure : sociology's essential
insights / Lynn M. Mulkey.
        p.   cm.
    Includes bibliographical references and index.
    ISBN 0-205-14881-6
    1. Sociology.   I. Title.
HM51.M783   1995
301—dc20   94-49567
                                                           CIP

Printed in the United States of America

10 9 8 7 6 5 4 3 2 1   00 99 98 97 96 95

Excerpts from *Sociology of Education: Theoretical and Empirical Investigations* by Lynn M. Mulkey, copyright © 1993 by Holt, Rinehart and Winston, Inc., reprinted by permission of the publisher.

For Anna

For self-consciousness, then, otherness is a fact, it does exist as a distinct moment; but the unity of itself with this difference is also a fact for self-consciousness, and is a second distinct moment. With that first moment, self-consciousness occupies the position of consciousness, and the whole expanse of the world of sense is conserved as its object, but at the same time only as related to the second moment, the unity of self-consciousness with itself. And, consequently, the sensible world is regarded by self-consciousness as having a subsistence which is, however, only appearance, or forms a distinction from self-consciousness that per se has no being. This opposition of its appearance and its truth finds its real essence, however, only in the truth—in the unity of self-consciousness with itself. . . . Self-consciousness presents itself here as the process in which this opposition is removed, and oneness or identity with itself established.

—G. W. F. Hegel, "Phenomenology" in *Hegel: The Essential Writings*

CONTENTS

5 WHAT WE WANT AND WHAT WE GET
Seeing Stratification as Social Structure 57

6 DEVIATING FROM WHAT WE'RE TAUGHT TO WANT, GET, AND BE
Seeing Social Control as Social Structure 69

7 CHANGING WHAT WE WANT, WHAT WE GET, AND WHO WE ARE
Seeing Social Change as Social Structure 79

PART II UNSEEING SOCIAL STRUCTURE
Being Fully Human through Cooperation 91

8 PERSONAL FREEDOM FROM SOCIAL DETERMINISM
Being in Society but Not of It 93

9 YOU'VE GOT THE WHOLE WORLD IN YOUR HANDS
Changing the Individual, Not Society 107

10 SOCIOLOGY
Ageless and Always New 119

PREFACE

Self-consciousness has before it another self-consciousness; it has come outside itself. . . . First, it has lost its own self, since it finds itself as an "other" being; secondly, it has thereby sublimated that other, for it does not regard the other as essentially real, but sees its own self in the other.

It must suspend this its other self. . . . It must set itself to suspend the other independent being, in order thereby to become certain of itself as true being.

—G. W. F. Hegel, "Phenomenology" in *The Philosophy of Hegel*

Any introduction to something—sociology, in this case—typically informs us about what to expect, but when we have many introductions to the same thing and they each tell us to expect something different, it's time for an introduction to introductions.

For me, it seems that sociology has become profane, sterile. We have lost touch with the soul of the field, with its powerful and profound and fundamental insights. We have become alienated in our experience of how society is the alphabet whereby we are written and how being human is impossible without society. We study society mainly as if it were something separate from ourselves. For at least two centuries, we have represented, participated in, and studied various features of individual and collective living; we have tried to accomplish model social orders of humans and society. Some social thinkers have addressed the issues of collective life—of war, crime, poverty, mental and physical pathology—by advocating changes to society. But this approach has simply reproduced the world it has attempted to change. This book introduces the perspective that collective problems are created by individuals—reflections of their attitudes and urges. When we realize this, we also realize that we haven't seen the world for what it is but only our projection of it. It follows logically that changing what we see changes the world—hence, "seeing social structure." Human society is a matter of individual development.

Recently, one of my students from India presented a paper on the social function of male virginity, and during the presentation, one of my American students raised his hand and asked, "But Dr. Mulkey, women actually do physically lose their virginity, don't they?" I said that I lose bacteria every time I brush my teeth, but so what? Nothing in our human experience has an inherent meaning until we give it meaning. Values tell us what things to pay attention to and how to feel about them; norms define behaviors that reflect these values. We embody social instruction.

For nearly ten years now, I have asked graduating seniors with majors in sociology to tell me, in a few words, what sociology is about. I hear, recurrently, explanations such as "It's about groups," "It's about interaction," "It's about social class," "It's about race," "It's about gender," "It's about occupations," and "It's about social issues." None of these students has clarified (to my satisfaction) what sociology is about.

Until recently, I, too, have been unable to convey what I know to be sociology's essential insights. My growing confusion about how to make sense of my own human experience, using available definitions of sociology, has been the very occasion, my challenge, for rendering an enhanced version of sociology. I would like to share with you what I *see*. This book introduces introductions to sociology. I introduce to you sociology as *seeing* and *unseeing* social structure.

FOUNDATIONS OF THIS BOOK

The American Sociological Association's *Footnotes* announced, in the words of Herbert Gans,[1] that sociology's virtues need calling attention to these days. Likewise, talk of crisis in sociology is in the air, and cost-cutting academic administrators are looking for departments to target for elimination. Perhaps sociology has gone unacknowledged mostly because it has not been articulate in identifying its contributions. In this book, I have attempted to evoke not the power of sociology but the perception or realization of its power.

In a combination of plain and sophisticated talk, this book ventures past some of the conventional yet somewhat artificial boundaries between disciplines. Using traditional labels, this book contains predominantly elements of traditional functionalist and conflict sociology as well as elements of social constructionist and humanistic sociologies. Ultimately, however, this work integrates extant sociologies.

Seeing and Unseeing Social Structure introduces sociology as having two equally important roles by emphasizing its significance for *both* the study of the social determinants of human behavior and, in this study, the realization of human subjectivity. As a *scientific understanding* of human social nature, the project consolidates the many theories of sociology around a more determinate level of observation—*principles of sociology*. Also, atheoretical empirical work is absorbed into a coherent analytical framework. As a *humanistic endeavor*, an understanding itself, the project demonstrates that by illuminating the social grounds of human identity, it is possible to develop an awareness, subjectivity, and individuality otherwise unavailable. The implications of reformulating the definition of sociology as a discipline are major—for teaching, for problem identification in research, and for practical application in the resolution of societal and individual problems.

My colleagues, misunderstanding me, say "So what? So what if we know that humans behave according to their internalized rules of the group? Big deal!" Let me try to articulate further why, for me, the dual contributions of sociology are such a big deal.

On my way to my first jog at the New York University Jerome S. Coles Sports and Recreation Center track, I got on the elevator going to the roof level, and when the elevator stopped at "R," the door would not open. I kept pushing buttons and looking for more buttons in my search to get the door to open. In one of the moments of my lost composure, I noticed out of the corner of my eye that the elevator door had opened behind me. I had not let the prospect that the elevator might have two doors enter my awareness, and by restricting my reality to one door, I had confined myself to one door with all its problems. I could have tried forever and never been able to get that one door to open.

This experience is a metaphor for my experience with sociology. In the past, I had restricted my experience of sociology by confining it to one understanding, but then I realized that, like the elevator, sociology has a second "door."

A second "door" is missing for the stockbroker who takes her life when the market crashes. She is so preoccupied with one reality, one way of being in the world, that it constitutes the only self she knows. When we do not conceive of another way of being in the world, we have no options to change our behavior.

Seeing and Unseeing Social Structure exposes, through scientific observation, how we limit ourselves to the experience of one "door"—how the regularities and determinants of our everyday human activities remain beyond our normal vision. *Seeing* is a realization, an awareness, a consciousness of how our behavior is constrained by others through shared rules for cooperative living (social structure), and by seeing, we move to a new level of human development. That is, by becoming aware of society's power to confer upon us a *social identity*—and thus a sense of meaning and direction in our lives—we are able to experience a fuller identity that can change society. Each identity has a set of consequences for our being in the world. The first identity, or self, *equates* itself with its social role, and the second self *expresses* itself through its social role. Socially assigned identities like "race" do not need defense as much as they need questioning as points of our attention in the first place. The former is a frenzied existence of social self-defense, and the latter is a peaceful and stable mode of being.

This is a timely work, not strictly because it exposes social influences on our behavior but also because it does so at a time when these influences are very much disguised from our sight. For Americans, seeing social structure is a peculiar challenge because of our society's focus on the notion of the *individual*. Ironically, social structural determinants of human behavior are beyond the vision of Americans, mainly because each person thinks she determines her own behavior. Ironically, in a country that defends the individual rights of life, liberty, and the pursuit of happiness, the lives of its members are governed mostly by a force beyond their awareness—the group. While the average U.S. citizen is likely to feel in charge of her life, she wouldn't even know why. Science and technology have advanced to the place where possibility has replaced imagination. A fetus may develop in an artificial womb, and women may be relieved from childbearing responsibilities. Humans may replicate life or find it in another universe, but they rarely question who they are in doing these things.

In addition to being a timely contribution, *Seeing and Unseeing Social Structure* is also a classic contribution in the sense that it introduces, in a new format, the distinctive analytical equipment needed for investigating the group's influence on our behavior. It presents a scientific perspective and concepts that are integrative and therefore enduring across *sociologies*—the diversity in the discipline of how social scientists conceptualize what they study that makes it difficult to teach sociology's essential insight. More simply put, major forms, or *principles*, of human cooperation (organization, stratification, social control, institutions, socialization, and social change) organize the many *theories* that attempt to explain their dynamics in past, present, and future terms.

George Ritzer foretells the emergence of a classic perspective of this type for representing what is uniquely sociological and why this emergence would be significant. He feels that eventually, there may be a new sociological paradigm that encompasses many sociological theories and takes into account the dialectical relationship between microscopic (individual/personality) and macroscopic (society) social phenomena. Should this new paradigm and its theories develop, they would not replace existing paradigms and theories but rather supersede them in being able to comprehend all types and levels of social phenomena. Note that this paradigm is posited for heuristic purposes and also as a theoretical model for empirical verification, evaluation, and specification.[2] The generic concepts of the perspective are a framework for analysis as they interpret the real-life experiences of individuals. In this manner, *Seeing and Unseeing Social Structure* is ageless and always new, a work that can be studied or read.

Sociology's focus on groups stresses social determinism and diminishes the significance of sociology's second but essential role in fostering the realization of individual freedom. Someone needs to complete what seems to be an unfinished story about the importance of sociology as *both* the study of how others influence our behavior and, as a study, an awareness that facilitates seeing social structure—the development of what it means to be individual in society.

◆ EXTANT LITERATURE: GAPS IN INTRODUCTIONS TO THE FIELD

Teaching Sociology (a journal of the American Sociological Association) documents the various and many standard introductions to sociology available in the college publishing marketplace. I'm interested in a much smaller group of books, which I'll call *introductions to introductions*.[3] I'll further reduce the category to include two books that come closest in purpose to that of this book: Earl Babbie's *The Sociological Spirit: Critical Essays in a Critical Science* and Peter Berger's *Invitation to Sociology: A Humanistic Perspective*.[4]

Babbie's work is an inspired presentation of the twofold contribution of sociology, but his notion of human freedom as an avenue for social change is different from that of Berger. Babbie believes that freedom is "in the world"; Berger solves this problem by designating the realm of human freedom as being outside society and having consequences for society. Some part of us is not socialized or transformed into social identity; this remainder of *unsocialized self* is regained in individual consciousness, so that persons are free from identifying wholly with their social roles.

Although Berger documents the source and nature of human freedom, more can be said about what happens once we are, in consciousness, *back in the world and not of it*. For example, freedom means looking past the ghetto child's race or poor educational performance and making provisions in educational policies based on a vision of freedom, not determinism. Persons are more than their roles and, in seeing that, are free to make society a reflection, rather than a determinant, of human potential.

◆ FEATURES OF THIS BOOK

This book addresses the general need for an introduction to introductions of sociology that is concise yet comprehensive in its statement of sociology's contributions. *Seeing and Unseeing Social Structure* gives equal importance to both dimensions of sociology: (1) as an understanding of the human social condition and (2) as a way of thinking about the world, a step in the development of human subjectivity.

Several strategies have helped me implement my program for a meaningful presentation of sociology. This book:

- Highlights sociology's dual role by apportioning the first part of the overview of the field to social determinants and the second to the realization of individuality.
- Uses current and actual student testimonies about a wide variety of social issues—the impact of society on their lives and the impact of their lives on society—to illuminate the social determinants of human behavior. Social issues are presented as nothing more than the collective representations of individual issues of identity and self-development.
- Introduces a unique, guiding conceptual framework for examining the social determinants of human behavior. The many sociological theories are integrated as levels of human consciousness and explanations of the operation of the principles of social life. Several audiences are accommodated by this introductory book; it has appeal as a supplement to other resources in any undergraduate and graduate course in sociology.
- Establishes relevance to daily living using colloquial language and real-life examples.[5] Chapters are introduced or include examples from literature, the news, and personal narratives to illustrate social forces, demonstrating the connection between academic scholarship and practical application.
- Includes examples that explicate the sociological insight, helping students see (experience) social structure. For example, students become conscious of their social selves and realize they are not their grades, body, friends, IQ, income, and so on.

◆ ACKNOWLEDGMENTS

This book is my second, but I continue to be unclear about where to begin when it comes to acknowledging the many persons who have, in one way or another, contributed to its development. As with my first book, it would take a detailed history of ideas to document how various individuals have influenced the evolution of the work. I smile when I think of Peter Berger; his articulation of a humanistic sociology has been revised as my formulation of sociology. The ideas of G. W. F. Hegel, Harold Garfinkel, and Joseph Campbell have taught me to focus less on what I see and more on what makes seeing possible in the first place.

Again, I suppose I should continue the applause by thanking my students at Hofstra and UCLA, who, in their quest for knowledge and good grades, sought from me clarity on the subject matter of sociology. Then I am especially indebted to Karen Hanson, Allyn and Bacon's Sociology Editor, for never doubting the contribution of this project. Sarah Dunbar, Annette Joseph, and Susan Freese saw to all the details involved in turning this project into a book. I also thank the following reviewers for their confirmation, not their affirmation, of the need to re-examine sociology as a field of study: Robin Franck, Southwestern College; Nils Hovik, Lehigh County Community College; and Rita Weisbrod, Augsburg College.

I continue to attribute my reexamination of the field of sociology less to the influences of my position in social structure and more to that Hegelian movement in my consciousness where, as sister, daughter, friend, or lover, my life becomes life living me.

NOTES

1. Herbert Gans, "Some Virtues of Sociology," *Footnotes* (Official Newsletter of the American Sociological Association) 20, no. 9 (November 1992): 4–5.
2. Lynn Mulkey, "The Relation of Principles to Theoretical Logic in Social Thought: A Re-Examination of a Field of Study," paper presented in the regular theory session on the history of social thought at the annual meeting of the American Sociological Association, Miami Beach, Florida, August 1993.
3. The following perhaps all qualify as and represent introductions to introductions to sociology: Peter Cookson and Caroline Persell, *Making Sense of Society* (New York: HarperCollins, 1992); Alan Johnson, *The Forest for the Trees: An Introduction to Sociological Thinking* (Fort Worth, TX: Harcourt Brace Jovanovich, 1991); Lorne Tepperman and Angela Djao, *Choices and Chances: Sociology for Everyday Life* (Fort Worth, TX: Harcourt Brace Jovanovich, 1990); and Anthony Gradens, *Sociology: A Brief but Critical Introduction* (Fort Worth, TX: Harcourt Brace Jovanovich, 1987). The first two are primers in how to think sociologically and investigate the various social factors that influence individual behavior. The third ties the theoretical discussions usually found in larger, comprehensive textbooks to the everyday concerns of students. None of these treatments addresses the dual role of sociology as an understanding and as an awareness that has consequences for the realization of human freedom from social determinism—

the final concern of sociologists, what it means to be an individual in relation to the group.

4. Peter Berger, *Invitation to Sociology: A Humanistic Perspective* (New York:
Doubleday, 1969); and Earl Babbie, *The Sociological Spirit: Critical Essays in a
Critical Science* (Belmont, CA: Wadsworth, 1994).

5. The value of this approach is discussed in L. Tepperman and A. Djao,
Choices and Chances: Sociology for Everyday Life (Fort Worth, TX: Harcourt
Brace Jovanovich, 1990).

SEEING AND UNSEEING SOCIAL STRUCTURE

PART

I

SEEING SOCIAL STRUCTURE
Becoming Human
through Cooperation

1 YOU CAN SURVIVE IF YOU COOPERATE
The Role of Sociology in Seeing and Unseeing
Social Structure

2 WANTING AND BEING WHAT OTHERS TELL
US TO WANT AND BE
Seeing Socialization as Social Structure

3 DOING WHAT OTHERS TELL US TO DO
Seeing Organization as Social Structure

4 DOING WHAT OTHERS TELL US TO DO
Seeing Institutions as Social Structure

5 WHAT WE WANT AND WHAT WE GET
Seeing Stratification as Social Structure

6 DEVIATING FROM WHAT WE'RE TAUGHT TO
WANT, GET, AND BE
Seeing Social Control as Social Structure

7 CHANGING WHAT WE WANT, WHAT WE GET,
AND WHO WE ARE
Seeing Social Change as Social Structure

*P*art I of this book is about sociology's fundamental activity as an awareness of and a technique for understanding how our behavior is affected by other people through laws of constraint (organization, socialization, stratification, social control, social change, and institutions).

We are made by the rules we make. Each new generation of humans takes on the group's instructions for cooperation, and society virtually becomes embodied in the individual as personality. The significance of sociology as an analytic tool for helping us understand why people behave the ways they do lies in its distinctive shift in emphasis from individual to group determinants of behavior. For example, a sociologist might expect that, according to the principle of organization, individual behavior is affected by the rules that specify how people who constitute a group should relate to accomplish a particular task. Some sociologists who attempt to explain how the principle of organization operates have theorized that, when a group is characterized by rules for formal organization (as opposed to informal organization), the relations between persons are segmented. For example, according to the rules for the group "students" (your individually learned attributes of being a student), you are unlikely to tell the person sitting next to you in class what you had for breakfast and whether you brushed your teeth this morning.

To critically understand the nature and effect of social forces (or principles) on people's lives, you will be introduced to each aspect of social scientific inquiry. The principle of stratification (rules for acquiring the desirable things in life), for example, operates when a society values a particular job and few persons have the skills necessary to perform it; society will motivate persons to fill that job by guaranteeing them more wealth, power, and/or prestige. In other words, people make their way in life on the basis of merit. This theory is supported by research from the U.S. Bureau of the Census, which reports that, on average, the group of highly educated persons is characterized by a higher level of income than the group of persons with lower levels of education. We employ such logic (theory) and empirical methods (research) in studying how others affect our conduct.

While sociology is the scientific study of the social determinants of human behavior, it is also a way of thinking about the world that itself has consequences for the development of individuality. Sociology conveys a major concern for the scientific investigation of groups and, in so doing, obscures its latent but primary concern with the individual; one can be individual only by taking others into consideration. The inevitable questions of sociology, then, are: How much are we free to act individually, and what does it mean to be an individual? Individuality is available to those who see social structure.

Chapter 1, "You Can Survive If You Cooperate: The Role of Sociology in Seeing and Unseeing Social Structure," will distinguish sociology as a special kind of inquiry by defining the concept "social" as it is used by sociologists and will show the relevance of this concept for understanding human behavior. In sum, this introductory chapter must account for two fundamental dimensions of sociology: what and how it studies and the consequences of this scientific understanding for what and how it studies. Sociology is depicted specifically in terms of three attributes:

1. Its subject matter: social phenomena or social structure (forms of cooperation, the principles of sociology)
2. Its scientific (logical and empirical) approach to knowing
3. Its ability, as a way of thinking, to advance each of us to an identity that changes the very society that created us

Chapter 2, "Wanting and Being What Others Tell Us to Want and Be: Seeing Socialization as Social Structure," discusses how society determines who we are. Emphasis is placed on how society, as the subject or determinant of our behavior, creates a social self (personality) via role prescriptions (that constitute objectified society) and the dynamics of internalization. Chapter 3, "Doing What Others Tell Us to Do: Seeing Organization as Social Structure," offers insight into the everyday need for formal and informal arrangements into groups. Chapter 4, "Doing What Others Tell Us to Do: Seeing Institutions as Social Structure," makes visible the collective expectations of society that act as constraints on individual behavior.

Chapter 5, "What We Want and What We Get: Seeing Stratification as Social Structure," presents the marked ways in which some people have more than others and why. Chapter 6, "Deviating from What We're Taught to Want, Get, and Be: Seeing Social Control as Social Structure," demonstrates that what the individual considers normal does not belong to him personally but to the society that decides what is normal. Chapter 7, "Changing What We Want, What We Get, and Who We Are: Seeing Social Change as Social Structure," illustrates the range of variation in society's prescriptions for behavior. It discusses the limited capacity for individual freedom found in society and reveals how social problems emerge from the perception of the self as a social self. Social problems are not so much problems but opportunities for realizing newfound perceptions of self and thus solutions to social problems.

YOU CAN SURVIVE
IF YOU COOPERATE
The Role of Sociology in Seeing
and Unseeing Social Structure

◆ SEEING THE ORIGINS AND NATURE OF COOPERATION

Sociology Is More about Individuals Than about Groups

Self-Preservation through Cooperation: *The Dancing Bees*

◆ SEEING AS THE SCIENTIFIC STUDY OF COOPERATION

Sociological Principles as Major Forms of Cooperation and Theories Explaining Them

How Society Makes Us: An Ego Sociology

◆ SEEING THE STRUGGLE FOR COOPERATION

Constraint as a Precondition for Freedom

From Self-Preservation to the Preservation of Selflessness

*M*eet Anna. She is not who you might think she is, and, more importantly, she is not who *she* thinks she is. She is not an *individual* as much as she is *society*. She is a human.

To understand Anna, you must know something about the other humans with whom she lives on the planet Earth. Fundamentally, Anna is amorphous protoplasm. *Society* is embodied as her *personality*—the consolidation of the group's instructions about how she should feel and act toward people and things in the world. Some instructions are "daughter" instructions; other instructions are "student" instructions, "girlfriend" instructions, and the like. Anna is aware of these instructions only as *herself*. She perceives her feelings and actions as inherent, natural, belonging to her. But Anna first belongs to society. She is the fish in the ocean; we understand the gill and the fin only when we understand the sea. Thus, we understand Anna only when we understand society.[1]

5

Moreover, if Anna is society, then what is *individual* about her? Once we are able to *see* society as Anna, then what will come into view is a new perception that enables us to *unsee* society—the realization of what it is to be an individual. The understanding of ourselves as two selves (the first self as society) has peculiar relevance for our being in the world, for our personal happiness, and for society and social problems—poverty and homelessness, depression and mental illness, suicide, drug addiction, crime, war. Changing the world and its problems happens when we change our *perception* of the world and its problems. That is what sociology is about—two new perceptions.

Any introduction to something—to sociology, in this case—typically informs us about what to expect. But when we have had many introductions to the same thing and they have each told us to expect something different, it's time for an "introduction to introductions."

In a statement made to my fellow sociologists of the American Sociological Association about the significance of sociology, I stated:

> *For years now, nearly ten, I have asked graduating seniors with majors in sociology to tell me, in a few words, what sociology is about. I hear, recurrently, "It's about groups." "It's about interaction." "It's about social class." "It's about race." "It's about gender." "It's about occupations." None, yes, none have articulated to my satisfaction, any clarity on what sociology is about, and I, too, until recently, have been unable to convey what I know to be sociology's essential insights. My growing confusion about how to make sense of my own human experience using conventional definitions of sociology has been the very occasion, my challenge for a better vision. I would like to share with you what I "see."[2]*

This book introduces introductions to sociology. I introduce sociology to you as seeing and unseeing social structure. *Seeing* refers to our becoming aware of the human as a social organism, a person who must take others into account for his own survival. The human survives by cooperating or agreeing with others about how to fulfill his needs. The agreements the human makes are recurrent and become the foundation for how he gets around in the world; we know them collectively as *society* and individually as *personality*. Once we come to see that personality is virtually society embodied in us as individuals, we grow in the recognition of two aspects of being human: the social aspect and the ground of our being (which makes the social aspect possible in the first place).

We become less attached to the social aspect, or personality. We do not hold onto society—the ego—with the same tenacity because it is not ultimately and completely who we are. Seeing is a step in the development of who we are. This realization is significant for our individual as well as for society's well-being.

SEEING THE ORIGINS AND NATURE OF COOPERATION

We know so little about ourselves. We act unaware of the determinants of our behavior—behavior that we feel is our own. For example, we just wouldn't feel comfortable walking across the street and into a house without knowing who lived there, let alone opening the refrigerator and pouring ourselves a glass of milk. Why not? Likewise, we just wouldn't grab (or even want to grab) a person walking past us on the way to the market and jump into the bushes to copulate. Why not? We just wouldn't feel right to give someone other than our biological mother or spouse our dirty underwear to wash. Why not?

We pay attention only to what society says is important. Thus, our seemingly automatic responses to the world are really not ours in the way we commonly experience ourselves. What seems to be ours is actually the group's. Society is the aggregation of instructions about how we should feel and behave. These instructions represent cooperation—*social structure*—or shared agreements about how to ensure the survival and well-being of every member of the group. Sociology, then, studies social behavior, which means it describes and explains society, or the rules of the group. But to get a good look at society, we must examine its manifestation, which is individual personality.

We can understand society by looking at, for example, Jennifer. The rules are not external to the individual as much as they are embodied as personality in Jennifer. Personality is nothing more than the organization of society via the individual's mechanisms of cognition, emotion, will, and sensation. Society is a set of instructions on how to employ all of these predispositions, which are reflected as preferences, disgusts, ambitions, and fears—when and how to prefer or to feel disgusted, ambitious, or afraid.

Meet Jennifer. She is society.

I can remember the first time that my mother shaved my legs for me. I was so excited I could not wait to feel my own smooth legs. I also remember looking at my underarms and trying to convince my mother that even though she could not see any hair, that I could, and I really needed to start shaving. It makes me laugh to think about how excited I was to shave.[3]

We will meet Jennifer again later and see how her judgment of herself is, in fact, society's judgment of her. Conversely, if we want to learn about society, the best way is to find it as personality.

Sociology Is More about Individuals Than about Groups

Sociology is a distinctive approach to understanding what Jennifer is about, what being human is about. Nonetheless, the term *sociology* has had many definitions. I define what sociologists study as *social* phenomena. A *social* phenomenon is any way in which other people influence our behavior through constraints on how we are to think, feel, and act.

This tidy definition counters others' claims of what sociology is about, especially those who emphasize that sociology is the study of groups:

> *Books on sociology have nothing clear to say about what the social is, about what society is. Even worse: not only do they fail to give us a precise notion of what the social is, of what society is; but, reading these books, we further discover that their authors—our esteemed sociologists—have not made any serious effort to clarify—even to themselves, let alone to their readers—the elementary phenomena in which the social fact consists. This is not to say—far from it!—that in these books, as in some others, there are not insights, at times inspired insights, into certain sociological problems. But, for want of clarity in regard to the fundamentals, these happy discoveries remain secret and hermetic, inaccessible to the ordinary reader. To use them, we should have to do what their authors did not do: try to clear up these preliminary and fundamental phenomena; hold ourselves resolutely to defining what the social is, what society is. Because their authors did not do this, like inspired blind men they sometimes manage to touch upon certain realities—I might say, to bump into them—but they do not succeed in seeing them, still less in clarifying them to us. . . . Thus it is that the ineptitude of sociology, filling people's heads with confused ideas, has finally become one of the plagues of our time. If this is so, do you not think that one of the best ways of not wholly wasting our time would be to devote ourselves to clarifying, to some extent, what the social is, what society is? . . . So, once again, let us set out in search of clear ideas; that is, of truths.*[4]

Although sociology's task has been to set forth the parameters of the human condition as a social condition, its arguments have obscured what is perceived as its central significance as a field of study. What clearly and concisely is the domain of social phenomena? What is the distinctive role of sociological thought, and how does it become visible when we ask the pivotal question in sociology: How much are we free to act individually, and just what does it mean to be an individual?

The term *social* refers to a concept, a mental image we use to classify aspects of our everyday experiences. The concept "hair" classifies aspects of the empirical world on the basis of similarities and dissimilarities from other aspects. When we consider Jennifer, what is sociologically interesting (or *social*) about her is how her behavior is less unique, arbitrary, and personal and more the result of constraints imposed by others; thus, we can make sense of who Jennifer is and what she does strictly by seeing her in relation to others. The whole group defines the parts of society, and the individual emerges from yet is inseparable from others. The group places a value on Jennifer according to an attribute it singles out, gives attention to, and names—"hair"—and then defines behaviors that reflect the value. Hairlessness is a cue to others about how to feel about Jennifer and how to act toward her. Jennifer's excitement over hairlessness is how she values herself, based on the group's values.

Sociologists identify six *principles of social constraint,* or ways in which others, through shared agreements for behavior, influence our individual behavior (discussed later in this chapter). Not only do these constraints determine our actions, but they make being human possible at all.

Self-Preservation through Cooperation:
The Dancing Bees

In the book *The Dancing Bees,* Karl von Frisch[5] describes the behavior of the honey bee, finding that bees have instinctual regulation of their actions in cooperating or taking others into account for their survival. The behavior of the queen in relation to the drone is governed solely at the level of instinct.

Human beings do not share this instinctual regulation. Through the capacity to build a self—a mental picture of oneself as an object, feeling and acting in specific ways according to how society decides—the human is able to subordinate organismic impulses to the control of social rules. What is a direct determinant in other organisms to the environment is mediated in the human by meaning assigned to the environment (culture). The human responds, then, not directly to the environment but to the meaning he assigns to the environment. Society embodies itself as these meanings, as the personality, the ego, or what the individual is aware of as its self.

in this saying that the ego is a direct response to culture?

In other words, humans have an enhanced adaptive capacity through culture to make seemingly arbitrary rules for cooperation. They make agreements on how to meet what the group identifies as human needs, and then they obey the rules. These agreements are *social facts* (prescriptions for behavior—when, where, and how to feel and act) that together compose *social structure* (rules as designated names for positions in the group and how to feel and act according to each position) and constitute the general body or *system of rules* (a set of interrelated parts) we shall refer to as *society.* Society is simply this set of agreements that exist externally to us and beyond our individual lives. Each society is a set of interconnected beliefs about how to go about living, and the very society that we create constrains us at the same time.[6]

Fundamentally, then, we are social creatures in that we must cooperate with others and agree collectively about how to survive. So while bees are also social creatures and take others into account and fulfill their own destiny according to genetically programmed instructions, humans are genetically programmed to make instructions. This evolutionary and adaptive capability gives humans the capacity to construct different "maps," or selves with different skills, to meet the changing demands of the environment. This is not true of many other animals. For example, a rat can run but will never compete in the Olympics.

By responding to the *meanings* we give to the environment and not to the environment directly, we are able to subordinate creaturely impulses. We are therefore less determined by the environment and have more dominion or freedom as agents of our own determination than do other organisms.

The vast number of permutations possible in the way individuals assign meaning makes sociology appear as an indeterminate scientific activity. Without exception, the rules determine the arrangement of individuals for accomplishing valued tasks (organization, stratification, social control, social change, institutions, and socialization), according to one inherent condition: the predisposition of the individual's interest in *self-preservation.* All other organisms depend directly on the process of biological evolution to adapt to their environments, but humans employ culture to adapt readily to varied conditions.

The human, in the name of self-preservation, has to defend the meanings for his behavior. That is why, in the name of self-preservation, Jennifer is anxious and unhappy when she doesn't shave her legs. Shaving her legs provides a predictable way for Jennifer to feel rewarded and secure in the world. Jennifer is her shaved legs, and by not having them, she feels less herself.

We will see, though, that this is not the final word about what makes us feel and act as we do. We will see that the optimum adaptation in self-preservation is the human's capacity for being independent from society—to be a self, a locus of control in the world—and for knowing that the self is actually indestructible.

SEEING AS THE SCIENTIFIC STUDY OF COOPERATION

We usually understand ourselves by thinking that we are free to act and choose who we are and what we do. But even though we are constrained by forces beyond our personal control—as in the case of our need for oxygen, without which we cannot live for more than minutes—our awareness is mostly of our individual identity and sense of voluntary action. Sociologists make us aware that what we do and are as human beings has meaning only in light of our association with what others in the same society do. Sociologists promote such an awareness by first specifying what they are observing as social behavior, or the rule-making and -following activities of humans. Sociology's first contribution is in delineating what it observes as well as the methods used for finding out how other people influence us. (This contribution is itself a social activity!) *stepping out of the box*

We are persuaded that we understand *reality,* how one thing affects (causes) another—for example, how lack of sleep is related to being tired. We are sure that we know, either through direct experience or from what someone else has told us, but often when we *think* we know, we actually do not.

Supposed you were talking with someone about men and women being paid the same income for the same job. You believe that women get paid less than men for performing the same job. The other person disagrees, saying, "The United States is a fair place, and everyone gets what he or she deserves." How would this argument hold up to logical and empirical verification?

Logically, sociologists would immediately recognize that the question of interest concerns the social principle of stratification (rules for acquiring the desirable things in life) and perhaps functionalist theory to explain how the stratification rules work. According to *functionalist theory,* if a society arranges for everyone to receive rewards of wealth, power, and prestige on a meritocratic basis, then females and males will receive equivalent salaries for the same occupations. An analysis of data from the 1990 *General Social Survey*[7] shows that women holding jobs of equal prestige as men get paid lower salaries. We thus reject the hypothesis that women and men make equal salaries for the same work, and we conclude that the United States is not such a fair place.

The point is that in order for us to really understand how we are affected by the social realm, we have to find out scientifically. Sociologists are concerned with both what they know and how they know it. The subject matter of sociology is social behavior, or the way others influence our behavior. Sociologists observe these phenomena scientifically, rather than casually, and can be confident in what they know because their observations are logical (things make sense; one thing follows another) and empirical (things can be verified by the senses of seeing, touching, etc.).

The logical part of science is called *theory,* and the empirical part is called *research.* The research process consists of beliefs and techniques that help scientists circumvent impediments to knowing. Researchers can avoid inaccurate observation by conceptualizing what they want to observe, putting the abstract concept into measurable form (for example, measuring the concept "happiness" as the number of times a person smiles per diem), and sampling a representative portion of the larger group to which findings will be generalized. Claims made about how sociological principles govern our activity are based on scientific observation.

Sociological Principles as Major Forms of Cooperation and Theories Explaining Them

Social phenomena act as major determinants of our behavior in that they are behavioral rules that constrain our behavior. We perceive their existence as independent of us and as having a structure or interrelatedness in a whole system of rules. When considered as instructions, social phenomena can be classified into more general types of rule-making and rule-following activities that specify how others influence us. Several principles explain how social phenomena (other people) affect our conduct.[8]

Six major categories or types of social phenomena appear universally (and operate simultaneously) to maintain order in all human societies. These social forces can be thought of as principles for making rules for living with other people. The six principles might also be thought of as five variations of the principle of organization *(rules guiding the arrangement of individuals into groups to accomplish a task). When human arrangements result in the transmission of the rules of society so that they become embodied in the individual as personality, we refer to the principle of* socialization. *When the arrangement specifies a pecking order as to who will get what of society's desirable things (wealth, power, and prestige) and under what conditions, we observe the principle of* stratification. *When the internalization of rules is asymetrical [sic] [variations in personality], humans arrange themselves in ways that bring conformity to the rules according to the principle of* social control. *The principle of* social change *operates as human arrangements that result in changes in the rules. The principle of* institutions *operates as human arrangements at the societal level that regulate major human functions (clusters of rules are directed toward a major task in the larger system; kinship rules for example, guarantee that society's members will care for the young).*[9]

These principles constitute the social realm that is open for scientific study—sociology. Sociologists devote their energies to finding out how and why these phenomena (as described in the principles) occur. The body of explanations of the nature and effect of each of these social forces is known as *sociological theory*. The many theories or systematic explanations put forth to explain the observed laws of the social realm are the many *sociologies*. Just as physicists posit wave and particle theories to explain light as a law or universal phenomenon, so do sociologists account for the operation of the principles governing rule making and following.

Although sociologists have identified what we are calling the general principles of constraint, many theories vie for prominence as systematic explanations for these observed laws. For example, we could explain why Jennifer feels badly when she does not shave her legs by using a theory of stratification. We know that people are ranked in all societies, but how do we explain why the result of such ranking is that some people have more desirable things in life than others?

One theory, the *functionalist theory*, explains the status of persons in terms of society's needs.[10] For instance, hairless legs serve as a designation of the value placed on women as nurturers. Women are valued as sexual objects and ultimately for childbearing and -rearing. Proponents of *conflict theory* reject the functionalist explanation and argue that female hairlessness is in the interests of an elite group whose wealth, power, and prestige are maintained by viewing women's importance as sexual objects.[11]

How Society Makes Us: An Ego Sociology

By the time we are two years old, we have taken on society. We have little say in how society achieves itself as us. The world already has been named and felt for us; this is a mother, a father, a sister, a brother (nominal designations or positions to play in relation to others and their accompanying pre- and proscriptions for action). This is good, bad, beautiful, and ugly. We learn these things so quickly and automatically that we forget that we actually learned them, that they were not already part of us.

Society as us is called our *ego.* The ego is the consolidation of society's rules. Our very disgusts and preferences are those of society. This locus of feeling and behavioral repertoire are now encoded as directions for how and under what conditions to emote, will, think (cognition), and speak (language). Even these concepts, such as "emote," are learned attentions to aspects of an otherwise undifferentiated world of experience. It is what each of us comes to know as *I.* It is an awareness of oneself being compelled to feel and act in certain ways in relation to given objects and persons in the world. This is why, as we shall see later, that when a family experiences dissolution, it is not something that happens "out there," external to the people involved. It is the breakdown of individuals, of their personalities, of their familiar ways of being in the world, of the I or of the ego. When the ego breaks down, it loses itself, seemingly so. We call that *depression,* which may even lead to suicide—the ego no longer knows how to be itself or what to do and feel in relation to others. The neurotic is simply someone who embodies conflicting values for how to feel secure in his encounters in the world. We shall discuss later, for example, how bulimic behavior is neurotic because it represents the negotiation of two internalized values: one on food for comfort and the other on thinness for self-worth.

The sociologist declares, then, that if we look at ourselves in a new way, we will observe that much of what we do is the result of forces beyond our personal control and free choice; social forces act on us with the same regularity as gravity. In seeing this, we can experience what it really means to be an individual—the difference between the *social self* and the *self* that makes the existence of the social self possible in the first place. The felt difference in this awareness of a *reductive* self to an *inclusive* self is analogous to the child who is secure by knowing that his mother has food and money in her handbag in contrast to the child who is secure simply holding his mother's hand.

◆ SEEING THE STRUGGLE FOR COOPERATION

Given that society creates the ego in each of us, our sense of security in the world depends on the felt intactness of our known ways for feeling and acting. Self-preservation in the human becomes a defense of those rules that society has become as us. If we have learned that having freckles is important, we count our freckles and defend their value. If we have learned that having long eyelashes is important, we do what we can to enhance our eyelashes. Other rules concern how we assign worth to our genitals; we call that *gender.* Still other rules concern our skin color, religion, cognitive development (i.e., idiocy versus genius), and more.

In a sense, we depend on society to tell us who we are—what's important and what to do about it. Logically, then, if we depend on society to tell us who to be in the world, then it determines us. Self-preservation is a matter of defending the rules that make us. We can see the relevance of the development of our social selves or egos; we are constantly oriented to self-defense, and we are happy when the rules are not threatened. For Jennifer, having hairy legs is threatening because society has declared that having clean-shaven legs ensures a predictable and rewarding response from others.

Constraint as a Precondition for Freedom

I'm not saying that our societally determined ego is all a mistake. Sociology is the scientific study of the social determinants of our behavior. Its systematic investigation of groups obscures its inevitable concern with the individual; one becomes individual by first taking others into consideration. Again, we return to the final question of sociology: How much are we free to act individually, and what does it mean to be an individual?

The scientific study of the social determinants of human behavior is an *idea,* a manner of thinking about the world, that itself has consequences for the realization of what it is to be an individual. According to the sociologist, the freedom to be fully individual is available to those who understand the social determinants of their behavior. Jennifer does not realize that she is not hairy legs, that they are merely one form of the expression of her being. It's as if we haven't really seen the world before; all we see is our learned way to pay attention to the world—our judgment of it. Sociology is thus the study of our judgments of the world.

From Self-Preservation to the Preservation of Selflessness

The epitome of adaptation, the hallmark of human evolution, is to realize that our personality (our social self, our ego) is an instrument for the *expression* of self but not the self per se. With this realization, we move to another orientation of our being, one that is relaxed, trusting, and not in defense of itself. Abraham Maslow refers to this state of awareness as the "intrinsic conscience beyond superego."[12] It is assured not by what it is or has become but by that which makes it all possible, and when one form of the rules is not available, it finds another. We come to see that we are not what we feel but that the feeling is already and miraculously us. We move away from disillusionment in the same way that we find out our parents are the tooth fairy. We lose nothing because it was never ours in the first place.

We can imagine the consequences of this orientation to being in the world: We share in everything but own nothing. The perfect society is achieved when just one of its members is free from self-defense. Such a person will create a society that reflects this new standard of self-giving.

In everyday terms, how does this kind of person look? My friend Meghan said to me that she was furious when someone called her an incompetent female. I said to her that in reacting, in feeling furious, she was asserting, in fact, that what the person said about her was true. A person who knows who she really is has no need to react and can exist in the world peacefully. It isn't that such a person doesn't acknowledge her need to be competent, but in grounding her sense of self beyond the material (physical) level and the social level, she does not worry about competence or self-affirmation. In letting go, she is more able to be competent without worrying about it.

Thus, in releasing the proprietorship or ownership of oneself, one finds oneself. When society is an addiction and we need it, we are concerned with the next "fix" instead of spontaneously living out what we are already.

Lévy-Bruhl says with truth that in primitive consciousness, the consciousness of the individual depends upon the consciousness of the group. But this is not the final truth about man. Society is a special reality, a degree of actuality. To regard man as exclusively a social being means slavery for man. The slavery of man to society finds expression in organic theories of society. . . . Society is presented as though it were personality of a higher hierarchical degree than the personality of man. But this makes man a slave.[13]

GLOSSARY

constraint An influence on us over which we have no control (determinism).

cooperation Rules for taking others into account for our own survival.

determinism Constraint on our behavior; a state of self-awareness that identifies itself with social rules (for example, the stockbroker who jumps out the window when the market crashes).

freedom A state of self-awareness that does not *identify* itself with social rules but *expresses* itself through social rules (for example, the person who feels like a worthwhile being regardless of whether he is wealthy, young, and attractive).

norm Behavior designated appropriate for reflecting a value placed on something.

perfection of cooperation The social structure that makes society a community of love; social rules and laws emanate from self-disinterestedness rather than self-interest; love subsumes the laws or takes others into account automatically.

preservation of selflessness An orientation to cooperation that is based on the assumption and felt security in the self apart from all of its social manifestations (for example, *I am* before I am a female, a mother, a daughter, a sister, a professor, a New Yorker).

science A socially achieved set of human relations based on values and norms for logic and empirical observation; causal thinking verified by sensory evidence.

seeing social structure Becoming aware of how society's rules are embodied as our personalities.

self-preservation An orientation to cooperation that is based on defense of the social self (for example, a person will defend himself as his race, his gender, his freckles, as if he *is* these things).

social phenomenon Any way in which other people influence our behavior through constraints on how we think, feel, and act.

social self The ego or personality; the consolidation of society's instructions in and as an individual's cognition and emotion (when and how to feel and think).

social structure A system of rules (society) for how we are to live cooperatively by taking others into account in order to promote our own survival; the rules exist externally to us and then become known to us as our personalities (how we think, feel, and act toward things and people in the world around us).

sociological principles Major forms of cooperation; major types of rules (values and norms) for living together, referred to as the principles of organization, socialization, stratification, social control, social change, and institutions.

sociological theories (sociologies) Explanations of how the principles of sociology operate.

sociology The study of social phenomena (all the ways others influence how we think, feel, and act); the science of the social determinants of our behavior; the study of the dialectical relationship of the individual to the group (others).

unseeing social structure Becoming aware of our social selves as necessary parts of who we are but not solely who we are.

value An abstract concept of judgment—"good," "bad," "right," "wrong," "disgusting," and "beautiful."

NOTES

1. This idea derives from Emile Durkheim's *The Rules of Sociological Method* (New York: Free Press, 1982, originally published in 1895), namely, his discussion of the individual as a representation of the group.
2. L. Mulkey and J. Wildeman, "The Closing of Sociology Departments: Changing Our View, Not the Dean's View," *Footnotes* (the Official Newsletter of the American Sociological Association), 22, no. 1 (1994): 7.
3. Reprinted with permission of the author.
4. José Ortega y Gasset, *Man and People*, trans. W. R. Trask (New York: W. W. Norton & Company, 1957), pp. 13–15.
5. Karl von Frisch, *The Dancing Bees: An Account of the Life and Senses of the Honey Bee* (New York: Cambridge University Press, 1951).
6. See note 1.
7. National Opinion Research Center (NORC), *General Social Survey* (Chicago: NORC, 1990 (J. A. Davis and T. W. Smith, principal investigators).
8. Reflexively, even principles are aspects of the empirical world that socially we name, judge, and act in correspondence to the judgment.
9. Quoted from Lynn M. Mulkey, *Sociology of Education: Theoretical and Empirical Investigations* (Orlando, FL: Harcourt Brace Jovanovich, 1993), pp. 13–14.
10. For one explication of functionalist theory, refer to Kingsley Davis and Wilbert E. Moore, "Some Principles of Stratification," *American Sociological Review,* 10 (1945): 242–249.
11. For one explication of conflict theory, refer to Randall Collins, "A Conflict Theory of Sexual Stratifications," *Social Problems,* 19 (1971): 3–12.
12. Abraham H. Maslow, "Various Meanings of Transcendence," in *The Farther Reaches of Human Experience* (New York: Penguin Books, 1971), p. 273.
13. Nickolai Berdyaev, *Slavery and Freedom* (New York: Charles Scribner's Sons, 1944), p. 102.

2

WANTING AND BEING
WHAT OTHERS TELL US
TO WANT AND BE
Seeing Socialization as
Social Structure

◆ BEING IN SOCIETY AND OF IT:
SOCIAL IDENTITY AS PART OF A TOTAL HUMAN IDENTITY

Reeboks Let You Be You

I'd Like to Introduce You to the Social Self: Durkheim, Marx,
Goffman, Mead, and Berger

◆ SOCIETY AS SUBJECT: ROLE ASSIGNMENT AND ACQUISITION

Getting Good Grades

Choosing a Mate or a Career Your Parents Would Like You to
Have

The Hand Is for Hanging Jewelry

*M*eet Jennifer. She is society.

*I can remember the first time that my mother shaved my legs for
me. I was so excited I could not wait to feel my own smooth legs. I
also remember looking at my underarms and trying to convince my
mother that even though she could not see any hair, that I could,
and I really needed to start shaving. It makes me laugh to think
about how excited I was to shave.*

*There is something else that sticks out in my mind. When my
best friend told me that I had a hairy stomach, that was all I could
think about. After all, girls are not supposed to have a lot of hair
anywhere except for their heads, and so I shaved that hair on my
stomach, too. But there was a difference between my wanting to
shave my legs and my wanting to shave my stomach. Every woman
I knew shaved their legs, and besides, it was "normal" to shave
your legs once you got to a certain age. But who shaved their stomach because their hair was too dark? And why did I care that the*

*hair on my stomach was darker than my friends'? And oh how
gross to have that hair on my stomach and then, the biggest moti-
vation for my concern—boys don't want girls with hairy stomachs.
So, . . . I placed a certain value on the hair that was on my body
and that decided for me how I felt about it. Why did the appearance of this hair bother me so much?[1]*

The principles of sociology central to this issue are socialization
and stratification. Persons are rewarded according to whether they
possess the characteristics society says are important. Persons also
come to judge themselves by society's standards. For example,
females are valued for hairlessness and are rewarded more power,
prestige, and wealth on this basis. And this group standard has
become part of how Jennifer feels about herself.

Society has accomplished itself as Jennifer. Society is not telling her
what to feel about herself; Jennifer is telling herself how to feel about
herself. Society has become Jennifer, and she has had no say in the
matter.

You might ask, Well, so what? But this self-knowledge has consequences for ourselves and for the society that styled us. We are each
human before we are male or female. Sociologists see *gender* as instructions about what to do with the genitals—how to value them and how
we should behave according to having one set of genitals versus the
other. I sometimes ask students to imagine what would happen if technology freed women from the responsibility of bearing children; the
fetus would develop in an artificial womb. Differences between men and
women in physical appearance, dress, and demeanor could be mini-
mized. Emotionally, men and women could be androgynous, and sexual attraction could be restricted simply to differences in genitals.
Hairlessness would have a different meaning or possibly no significance.

Remember, sociology takes what seems obvious and shows us that it
isn't. Sociology always asks of the human social animal, What if? It
understands that the world of experience for the human must be organized—named, judged, and acted toward. Some aspects of experience
never get our attention, even though they exist. I can't even illustrate
this point because I don't have words for things to which I haven't
learned to give my attention.   MYSTERIES

Think again that males and females could be alike; they would act
alike and feel alike. Both would be equally aggressive, affectionate, nur-

turing, and instrumental. Being human is impossible without having the instructions from other people for how to be human.

Socialization creates a blueprint or master plan for human behavior, and sociologists ask, Who makes these decisions and how? They also ask whether we identify with these designations, as ourselves, or whether we base our self-worth on the a priori experience of our being so that we express ourselves through these designations. What are the consequences for us and for society when we *express through* versus *equate with* society?

Seeing *socialization* as social structure means wanting and being what others tell us to want and be.[2] For organisms such as the African weaver ant (*Oecophylla longinoda*), genes determine its unique responsibilities in the colony; for example, the queen is specialized to lay eggs.[3] But we humans cannot find a gene that directly explains why Jennifer feels disgust at the sight of hair on her stomach.

> *For humans, the parameters of destiny are predictable in a different way; humans have the freedom to develop creative ways for cooperation, and in turn, are determined by their own instructions.[4] Humans are predestined by their genetic structure not simply to follow the rules encoded in their genes, but to make rules for living and then follow them. The human urge toward self-preservation is manifested as a predisposition or orientation to develop and conform to group rules as a mechanism to ensure the survival of each individual member of the group. Our template universally ordains participation in the activity of socialization (the learning of the values, knowledge, and skills of the group into which one is born [that is, one's family and society]) so that we learn not merely what other people believe, but we come to prefer what they believe.[5]*

We are, at this stage of human development, unable to distinguish the self as a conglomeration of learned preferences from the self that did the learning.

BEING IN SOCIETY AND OF IT: SOCIAL IDENTITY AS PART OF A TOTAL HUMAN IDENTITY

Don't be deceived. We're not who we think we are.[6] By way of the principle of socialization, the human response to the external environment is one that seems to that organism naturally the way things are. In other organisms, genetic prescriptions directly determine their behaviors. The configurations of human action come from external to internal, not internal to external. We have an enhanced flexibility of responses to the environment, yet we are disillusioned in experiencing the learned ways of feeling and acting toward things as directly as our own. But this is our social identity and only part of our total identity; it is imposed on our real identity, which existed before it but is knowable only after we see our social self, identity.

What is social about the human is that in taking others into account for her own survival, the human must take on the group's strategy about what she is to do with herself. This collective judgment is experienced by the human as her self—her personality, her personal or inner needs. That is why I get disgusted when I see a woman with hairy legs and underarms. It feels very much like *my* disgust, but really, it's *society's*. We come to want not through what is genetic but through what we are taught to want. And the property of *I*, my personality, is actually the manifestation of our essential sociality—the externally defined and internally conditioned regulations of our humanity. Undifferentiated matter is formed to the group image, a system of relatedness. But all this feels like "just me," the individual choosing her own manner of action.

The external shared directions necessarily are of certain types that organize persons internally in their orientation to others. The *principles of sociology* refer to these patterned forms of relatedness. This rule-making and rule-following proclivity and activity operates without exception in humans and human groups; it emanates from within the subjective consciousness of the individual and manifests itself as perception of an external society.[7]

The matter of sociological significance, then, is that the human hasn't been born, except as a predisposition; she is born at the end of a developmental sequence that includes her sociality. The evolution of incomplete to complete organismic experience is partially accomplished through a three-dimensional process that makes the human into her self.

According to Peter Berger,[8] the universal process of becoming a social being entails the dynamics of *externalization, objectification,* and *internalization.* Interestingly and remarkably, the very way in which I name the world—that is, tell you what might be a principle—is the very process of socialization. Aspects of the perceived world are noted, defined as worthy of our attention.

- When humans outwardly express their attention to some aspect of their experience, judge it as good or bad, and prescribe actions appropriate toward it, they are *externalizing*. What is inside the person becomes perceived as outside the person.
- When a rule residing inside an individual comes outside the person and is collectively held, society is produced in its own right

as an object; this is *objectification*. Society is nothing more than the consolidation of externally produced and collectively held judgments that have a constitution and a life that go beyond the individual. The rules of the group comprise society as the manifold individually externalized judgments. These judgments are comprehensive and go beyond the projections of any one person, yet any one person can come to "hear the whole symphony" even though it may represent only one part of the score.

- When the collective judgments as an object—society—become represented in the individual's consciousness, the human is the product of the group. This is *internalization*. Personality is a record in each person of the group's rules for behavior. The human has no inborn relationship to her surroundings; sociology is interested in the mechanisms whereby that relationship becomes established in the dialectical process of achieving the society that achieves us.

Let's talk a little about the juxtaposition of the social part of the person against the person who has a social part.

Reeboks Let You Be You

You've probably seen the advertisement for Reebok athletic shoes— "Reeboks let you be you." But society tells us, in this, who we really are, which is ironic because we are alike in that we all come to feel as if we are individuals. The misperception and misconception is that people feel mostly that they are in society when society is in them.

American society places a high value on individual rights. But without personality—this and other group prescriptions for how we should feel and behave (society)—we wouldn't know what to do with ourselves. For example, if the woman in front of you in line at the post office turned around and grabbed your money to pay for her stamps, how would you react? Society instills in us and as us rules that govern our actions. In this scenario, we have learned that according to our position in the group (stamp purchasers), we have specific obligations in feeling and acting. Society has *organized* (discussed in next chapter) our behavior so we can constitute members of a group. We have learned that only under certain conditions can others around us share or take monetary resources, yet, of course, we think our anger is justified and automatically so. So, when someone violates a rule and we can't make sense of what they are doing, we learn either to punch her in the nose or dismiss her as insane because she has gone against what we seemingly know as naturally the way things are.

Society constantly announces the so-called real you as the social you, but this is not the truth about you—at least, not totally. What feels like the real me—my disgust when I see someone picking her nose or when I pick my nose—is really disgust organized by society. This is the *thought* self, the self as it is known to itself and to others. We identify with who we are taught we are so that we can act cooperatively with others. But who we really are is defined by a state of nonself thought, or selflessness; this realization of self is itself part of our human development.

At this stage in development, *selflessness* emerges, not as the abolition of the self but rather as the abolition of the thought and defense of the self. It is unconditioned by thought and not limited by the laws and operations of thought. We are able to feel life living us as opposed to becoming imprisoned by social conditions for our happiness and success. For instance, because society says money is power, we feel powerful when we have money. If society said the number of hairs in our eyebrows indicated power, we would feel more or less respectful of ourselves and others on the basis of the number of eyebrow hairs.

It goes on and on, this business of identifying with thoughts that embody society's preferences. *Value* is a social concept; it is familiarity with ourselves solely in the way we are taught to view ourselves. We have lost the mystery of being creatures. It feels just the way it's supposed to when we walk past other people on the street. What is strange, what feels familiar, is that each is human; each stands erect, on two legs, has two arms and eyes, and the eyes are in front of the head. We have become known to ourselves in the ways we think about ourselves. This knowledge may be a necessary social function, but we forget that what is knowing and what is thinking is the fundamental self (and forgetting is part of the growth into expanded awareness of who we are). We have become reduced to our social thought. Consider my student who, when asked how he felt when he approached an 85-year-old, responded, "Well, that's a pretty worthless human being." We have been conditioned to feel, corresponding to age, the value of a human being, and we act out these feelings behaviorally—the aged are relegated to rest homes because they make few socially valued contributions.

Here's another example of personality as society's judgment. Joe is society as the shy personality:

> *All my life, I have wanted, just once, to meet someone without being introduced by a friend. . . . I can't approach a girl, introduce myself, and begin a conversation. . . . I start to break out in a cold sweat and start shaking. It's like a disease. . . . Every Tuesday and Thursday, I try to tell myself that I am going to . . . introduce myself to this girl in my English*

*class that I would really like to meet (and have for the last 10 weeks). . . .
I try to tell myself that I am going to do it, but I always chicken out. I
can't even figure out what I am afraid of. I will lose my chance because
the semester is almost over, and I will deeply regret not taking the initia-
tive. Why is it so hard for me to be sociable when I really want to be?*[9]

Joe is afraid of himself; he feels himself unable to be society in the
way it expects. We typically attribute such intimate feelings to ourselves,
when they belong first to society.

Bryan reviewed a study about differences in how men perceive and
react to thinning hair because he realizes now that he is his baldness. It
hardly seems possible that Bryan feels as he does about becoming bald
because society, for its purposes, has organized his feelings in this manner. Something so remote as society's prescription for being male
includes the quality of being hairy. Having hair has come to mean "good
looking," according to society's standards, "instrumental," "aggressive,"
as opposed to being smooth, being soft to touch as an *object*. The sociological insight and growth in self-understanding is in knowing we are
neither, or we "are," before we are either. *Employing* one's social identity
also has a different set of consequences than *becoming it*.

Bryan explains:

*As I approach my twenties, I have found myself spending considerable
time looking in the mirror. . . . I am very concerned about the status of
my hair. You see, my father started losing his hair in his early twenties. . . . Hairstyles may seem trivial and a waste of time to many males,
but to me, it is very important, and I often find myself judging others by
the way they wear their hair. . . . If I see a man with long, stringy hair, I
usually think of him as a "head banger." But most importantly, if I see a
person with a head of thinning hair, my reaction is that he is old and
unattractive; I feel sorry for him and think of how miserable he must be.
Balding is ugly in my book, and I am extremely fearful that this horrible
phenomenon, which has haunted my family for so many generations,
may eventually find its way to me!*[10]

Bob has become "the baseball player." He gives us yet another
glimpse of the consequences of knowing oneself solely as a social self:

*It has been nearly two years now from the last time I stepped onto a base-
ball diamond. Many people thought that I was a natural at the game.
Going back to my junior year, I even believed them. I was at the top of the
ladder. I had just been elected to the all-state team as a pitcher. My senior
year was going to be even better. One day when I was playing around, I*

tore cartilage in my knee. From that day forth, I never went on the dia-mond again. . . .

It wasn't the fears of the injury itself: I could have gotten back into shape. It was something else. I am really glad I did this paper because it finally made me deal with my problem. It took a lot of soul searching to figure out my problem. I still don't have all the answers, but now I am try-ing to figure them out. I feel that the biggest problem with myself is that I have to be the very best at whatever I do. I always worry about what other people think or say about me. I couldn't deal with the added pressure of being the best. I couldn't deal with the headlines saying how good I was and giving me all this praise. When I walked away from the game, it was like a heavy weight was lifted off my shoulders.[11]

As a final example, consider Joseph, who is pondering his social condition:

I remember sitting in a dentist's office and picking up a magazine. I turned to the back cover and began thumbing through the magazine, starting from the last page and working my way toward the first page. I stopped and began to wonder why I went through the magazine in such a fashion. I always do it, but now I was wondering why I always do it. Then it hit me. Local newspapers, such as the Post *or the* Daily News, *place the sports section in the very rear of the paper. Sports have become such an integral part of my life that it has become an instinctual (although actu-ally learned) act to pick up a magazine or newspaper and work from the back to the front. It would not be an exaggeration to say that my day begins, ends, and is filled with sports. I wake up, and I read the sports pages. During the day, I will play some type of sport (either physically or on a video game system). At night, I usually watch some type of sporting event, and before I go to sleep, I enjoy finding out about all of the day's sporting events on the evening news. It is not just curiosity or interest but rather a passion.*

Sports viewing can have an effect on my emotional and even my phys-ical state. I remember watching as my favorite boxer lost for the first time in his career. It was completely unexpected, and I was devastated. For days afterward, I would feel as if I were in another world. I couldn't concentrate on schoolwork, I wasn't eating much, and I would just sulk around. I can also remember watching my favorite team in the World Series. It was a tremendous rush of excitement and truly an experience that words could not describe. Such highs. Such lows. Such a big part of my life.

After coming to the realization that sports are a big part of my life, I was left asking myself many questions. Then, after picking up this study, I began to probe even deeper. What made me choose sports? . . . Masculine or feminine is what, with appropriate socialization, you become. Sports are approached, observed, and responded to differently by the different genders. Males are encouraged to be assertive, dominant, competitive, and vocal, while females are praised for being reactive, submissive, cooperative, and quiet. . . .

Part of the purpose of the socialization process is to ensure that men and women can form a workable union. By creating man and woman (not by birth but through socialization), we create diversity. This leads to a divergence in thought and emotion. A game that is truly important to a man can be, to a woman, an annoying reminder of a weekly ritual. It is ironic that, in the process of trying to get men and women together, the socialization process is also helping to drive them apart. This assignment and this course have opened my eyes to a new vision or perspective of things. Philosophy taught me to use logic and to think things through. Sociology has left me challenging all that I have come to be and all that I will become.[12]

Notice Joseph's point about how socialization separates men and women. When we identify with our social directions, then we are alienated from others on the basis of social differences. When we are able to see social structure, then we are able to be different from others socially but united with others by a different standard.

Remember that sociology makes visible the distinction between the social self and the real self. In doing that, it can make things different for us and society.

I'd Like to Introduce You to the Social Self: Durkheim, Marx, Goffman, Mead, and Berger

A lot of social thinkers have been preoccupied with that phase of our development where we are frauds. By getting to know ourselves as social selves, we are ready to experience our genuine state of self. Sociologists are experts on frauds, on documenting and theorizing on the formation and dynamics of the ego, essentially the program for functioning in the group. For many seminal thinkers, the individual is more or less but ultimately dependent on the group for who she is. For Emile Durkheim,[13] the social self is the individual representation of society, probably in the same way I say society is embodied in the individual as personality. For Karl Marx,[14] the social self is a state of self-consciousness determined strictly by a person's material value or economic relatedness to the group. For Erving Goffman,[15] the social self is the only self but is individual in how it varies its presentation of itself as social. For George Herbert Mead,[16] the human, via its mind, creates the self as an object and views itself acting and feeling according to society's prescriptions. For Peter Berger,[17] the experience of the social self is imposed on the self.

Don't get me wrong, here. Being a social self, or ego, is a necessary condition for our existence. When we identify totally with it (which we will talk about later), we are not complete in our development. Sociologists reveal how, through the principle of socialization as a form of organization, individuals arrange themselves into groups to transmit the rules of the group. As mentioned earlier, three arrangements (externalization, objectification, and internalization) accomplish the overall organization.

SOCIETY AS SUBJECT: ROLE ASSIGNMENT AND ACQUISITION

Each thinker admits to the inevitability of a human's reliance on others to know what to do with herself, but each answers the question of how and to what degree this human depends on the group to be herself.[18] In the history of the science of human behavior, Peter Berger is among those, including the author, who render the social realm as necessary, but not final, in the human experience of itself. Before we can understand this idea, we must be able to describe, with some semblance of precision, the fundamental recurrences of society as we perceive them "in" and "out" of us. We will investigate in greater detail the threefold nature of the principle of socialization.

We have rehearsed the basic thought of society as an object. Add to that thought a consolidation of rules, and the object has a *structure*. This means each rule is like a piece in a puzzle; it plays a distinct part in relation to the whole system of parts. Each piece or rule makes up society in the form of values and norms, specifically, *statuses* and *roles*—sets of behavioral directives. This template of rules orders our individual experience according to its place in a broader context of experience. To make sense of what we do, then, requires a look, simultaneously, at the complete puzzle and each piece that comprises it.

The principle of institutions is that feature of rule making that reflects how roles and statuses are part of a larger interrelated network, or system. Jennifer, for example, feels and acts according to her status: female (a position designated as part of a cluster of rules that create a relatedness between persons known as the institution *the family*). Her very personality, as it feels and acts as a female, represents the interests of society in preparing some of its members for nurturing behaviors.

Getting Good Grades

In asking about how the principle of socialization makes us do what we do, think about getting good grades. Everyone knows it's important to get good grades, but certainly no geneticist can locate a gene that dictates this knowledge. Society derives from humans but also comes to confront them as a condition of fact (sui generis) outside themselves.

Society, as a social phenomenon, cannot be found by self-reflection, just as one musician reflects but does not produce the whole symphony. The pride over a good grade and the discouragement over a bad grade feel fully our own, but society tells us under what circumstances we should feel and how.

Choosing a Mate or a Career
Your Parents Would Like You to Have

It's one thing to talk about society "out there," but when society is reflected in our choosing a mate or a career our parents would like us to have, that is another of society's real accomplishments. Recall that social structure in the form of statuses and roles is internalized in individual consciousness, and the various elements of the objectificated world are sensed as part of one's nature. Each new generation learns the behavioral prescriptions, and a successful socialization is one that results in a high degree of objective and subjective alignment.

The feelings of ambition and attraction are chiseled from an otherwise undifferentiated propensity to feel and act.[19] "Mate" is simply a category of behaviors, as is "career." We are, to the core, produced by the group. Mating, for example, is the styling of human sexuality; society says under what conditions to feel and act sexual—with whom, where, when, and how.

To take on society through the dialectical or reciprocal activities of externalization/objectification and internalization, the human depends on her capacities for language, cognition, and emotion.

Rule production and reception is the ability to form a judgment about what one is sensing—Is it good, bad, right, wrong?—to identify a feature of an experience, to name it, to place a value on it, and to order action in accordance with the meaning we give to experience. Identifying and judging attributes of our experience rest on our capacity to represent how we feel and how we act in symbols—language. We can anticipate the actions of others toward us and we toward them by sharing how we together want to treat and react to the world.

Humans are not directly influenced by their biology; how we act depends on our ability to record in our brains information about what we focus our attention on, how to feel about that we are attending to, and physically representing these feelings. The hand, for example, is directed to take a life or to save a life. What the group, or society, wants to attend to gets our attention, and other characteristics of our experience remain unattended. For example, for some humans, underarm odor goes unnoticed; in fact, there may be no such symbol as "underarm odor." Discriminating subtle differences in our attention may be required for survival in certain group environments; paying attention to small unit changes in temperature may affect the subsistence in a particular historical-geographical locale. For the human, the nose needs a mind to record in addition to sensation, a reference to it, what it means: Does it mean that we pay attention to odor? Is it an odor of a summer house and vacation activity? Is it good? Is it bad? Is it a worker-related sector of odor? Sense for the human must be signed symbolically noted, externalized and denoted, and internally registered and decoded in time, in judgment, and in behavior—what to do with it. A "good" tomato is firm and red when you want to make salad; it is mushy and moldy when you want to throw it at Professor Mulkey. These are the only ways we experience the tomato. Our sense is styled and relegated to a limited level of human experience.

Certain mental operators are foundational to translating our sensation of the world to symbols, meaning, and language. Our cognitive abilities allow us to recall information to order it in time, as *before* and *after,* and in space, as *here, there,* and so on. Jean Piaget[20] postulated that we organize the world in our heads in a developmental, stagelike sequence from concrete to abstract. A young child is limited in how she represents her mother's presence. Her cognition restricts her awareness of her to her visual presence. However, when cognitive ability develops to another level, the same child will represent her mother's presence simply by hearing her voice from another room in the house or the information that she is going to town and will return shortly. Classifying our experiences by naming and ordering them is part of the socialization process. Each detail of our sense world is managed by our cognitive facility.

The human capacity for emotion also develops through a process of social management. We are predisposed, developmentally, to emote, but the naming of these feelings and how and under what circumstances they will be expressed is a social achievement. Emotions emerge as comfort or discomfort; the five-year-old can experience empathy because she can perceive herself as separate from her surroundings. She can generalize feelings to whole groups by forming categories mentally, based on particular attributes of persons and things.[21]

The Hand Is for Hanging Jewelry

Naming the details of our experience and manipulating them in our minds via symbols allows us to record a version of society in us, and as us, because these notations order our predisposition.[22] Take the hand, for instance. Society tells us what to do with it and how to feel about it. In cognition, it names the feature, and in emotion, it governs our feelings. For some humans, the hand is "good" when it has polished nails and is covered with jewelry. The hand is thus a cue to others and for me about who I am: Here I am, hands; hands that are to be viewed as sexually attractive, to ensure society's need for reproducing the species.

The rules that order our behavior become encoded as our cognition and emotion in the form of values, norms, statuses, and roles. Society is thus a language system in that it is a collection of shared symbols that represent information about the world and what we should do with it. A *value* is a judgment about something, the feeling of whether it is right or wrong, for example. We are able to evaluate people, objects, and events as to their worth or worthlessness, merit or failure, beauty or ugliness, good or evil. A value is first a mental and emotional notation that becomes expressed behaviorally. There is no inherent relationship between myself and the environment—I must be told what to do with it. I first must be told to value it—to judge it as worthy of my attention—to pay attention to a person's skin color, but not to the number of hairs in her nose. A value is thus a notation in our emotion and cognition that something is important. How, then, do we act out the importance we assign to it?

Once we have in us a record of the value of an item, then we need the *norm*, the behavioral instructions that reflect the value. The apparent natural disgust that I find at the thought of eating my cat for dinner seems like another "so what?" sentiment. But our every action is explicable solely by instruction—to starve rather than eat cat. If we value something, it gains our attention; this is the initial phase in explaining human behavior. Then our emotional reaction sequences our response. The "cat," as a social achievement, has gained our attention, visually, and then in moral judgment. This is an organism we do not eat. Eating or not eating is the behavioral directive that mirrors the value. And there we have a socially constructed association of the human to the world.

The myriad of human responses that we take as our own are under the group's authority—our sexual attractions are organized to exclude persons by age, height, religion, and socioeconomic status. Every motion, so to speak, is socially contrived. The rules, social structure, and society are nothing more than a composite of values and norms. Values and norms are further structured into categories, statuses, and roles. The place or position in the whole is called a *status*, and the values and norms specific to that position are called *roles*. Human protoplasm is without direction until it is told "You are a spouse—love, honor, obey this other protoplasm."

The sum of our statuses is known as the social self, the ego, the personality. These abstractions are "the object" we become to ourselves. Unaware, we come to sense being a distinct locus of experience in all the ways we have been directed to feel and act. Our sense of compliance in this is our self-esteem—how well society has achieved its goals as us.

The principle of socialization accounts for how we establish our association to the world; unformed sensation becomes an ordered experience according to fitting the world into mental categories of action toward it. Our actions and others become predictable; this is how we become aware of or known to ourselves—through a select grid of behaviors. Society calls out in us and names certain feelings, defines behaviors that act out those feelings, when and how. This protocol of events makes an undefined person into a social person. This makes the runner who loses a leg at a loss of her socially defined self or a big-nosed and -breasted female less a self in a group that values persons with little noses and small breasts. This makes persons "surgeons," not by encouraging suppression of emotion but by encouraging nonemotion in certain contexts. This makes women content to embroider and men content in having sophisticated knowledge.[23]

This is why I say that sociologists are experts on the mechanisms of judgment and their accompanying and patterned behavioral objectifications. This is what I mean when I say that we haven't seen the world; we see only social structure and our learned judgment of it.

Sociologists study society, a set of rules for experiencing the world that we must share for our survival in the group. Each of the judgments we learn has consequences for our action; if a skinhead feels more valuable and better than other persons because she is White and has a particular curvature of the nose, then she will act out this value toward others. When our sexual urges expressed one way versus another are noted symbolically, our behavior becomes known as rape, conjugal rights, homosexuality, or date rape. It's all by design, but mistakenly, we take ourselves to be ourselves by our own choosing. We are the group.

Throughout this discussion, we have considered how our behavior is explained as the influence of others (although *influence* is not an appropriate word because being human is not possible without other people). Socialization is rooted in the human capacity for internalizing society as behavioral directives (values, norms, statuses, roles) through the vehicles of cognition and emotion (language and personality).

Although socialization enhances our capacity to develop adaptive modes of survival through assigning meanings to events (how, by definition, we will respond to things and they to us), we must ask who makes the rules and what aspects of being human are disallowed because of the rules. Society, in the last analysis, makes us addicts; we need society as a map of how to get around in the world. The predicament that logically follows concerns our dependence; we are virtually addicts until our identification with society changes. As a sociologist, you have acquired a new analytical tool—the principle of socialization. It is a clue to the anatomy and physiology of our sociality, and itself as an understanding, a step in the developmental sequence of becoming fully what we are.

Sociology is a special vision that allows us to see that we are society. Once we can see it, we can, so to speak, unsee it. We can recognize our oneness with society in the same way that we recognize that oxygen determines our existence, but we no longer need to worry about it because our life is neither in the oxygen nor in society but in the energies that made them possible. Identification with what makes seeing possible, not with the substance of what we see, changes our sense and way of being in the world.

Jennifer should be happy with or without hairy legs. But society has done such a good job on her that she feels like she is *in* society, when, of course, she *is* society. If we do a little sociology, we are inevitably going to confront ourselves by asking, Just who, then, in the world am I? What constitutes individuality and self-determination? Certainly not our fingerprints or physical differences or feeling good about ourselves when our legs are hairless. It is silly to think that it's my life; rather, life lives as me. Sociology's essential insights allow us two perceptions of what it means to be an individual, each with different consequences or relevance for society's well-being and, most of all, for our well-being.

GLOSSARY

externalization The process whereby a person expresses a rule for her action in relation to others.

internalization The process whereby a person is able to represent society's values and norms as her personality (cognition and emotion); in other words, she comes to prefer and do what society tells her to prefer and do. For example, Americans are disgusted by the appearance of women with hair on their legs.

norms A set of expected behaviors that represent or reflect a value. For example, the female is valued primarily for childbearing and -rearing responsibilities, and a behavior that reflects the value is hairlessness.

objectification The process whereby a rule for behavior (how to feel and act toward something) becomes collective, part of a consensus about how people as a group should act to survive; the rules are known at this phase as *society*.

personality A mechanism consisting of the human's inherent capacity for cognition and emotion that records in her the rules of the group of which she is a member; the unique representation of society as a set of prescriptions and proscriptions in the individual. The personality is also the social self, or the ego, and the fundamental way in which people experience who they think they are.

roles Social structure or rules; a set of values and norms specific to a particular social status. For example, the status "female" is acted out as a specific and assigned set of feelings and actions.

sociality The human organism's predisposition to taking on society; social nature; the ability to record society's values and norms in cognition and emotion.

socialization, principle of A process and form of organization whereby the human becomes known to herself as a social self; through externalization, objectification, and internalization, the individual acquires the directions for group living.

society as subject The group becomes the subject by telling her what to do with herself; people learn what to do with their feelings and thoughts, and this map is of society, a design for how people should interact; people come to know themselves initially in this way, as society.

statuses Social structure or rules; a designated position that one holds in the division of labor or the whole society. For example, the position "male" is represented by a specific set of values and norms.

values Abstract judgments of how to feel about things or people, such as good or bad, right or wrong, beautiful or ugly, and so on.

NOTES

1. Reprinted with permission of the author.
2. This paragraph has been adapted from Lynn M. Mulkey, *Sociology of Education: Theoretical and Empirical Investigations* (Orlando, FL: Harcourt Brace Jovanovich, 1993), p. 87.
3. G. Oster and E. Wilson, *Caste and Ecology in the Social Insects* (Princeton, NJ: Princeton University Press, 1978).
4. Documentation exists of the biological innateness of human social behavior. For example, see Mary Ainsworth, S. M. Bell, and Donelda Stayton, "Infant-Mother Attachment and Social Development: Socialization as a Product of Reciprocal Responsiveness to Stimuli," in P. M. Martin Richards, *The Integration of a Child into a Social World* (New York: Cambridge, 1974), p. 100. The epitome of the organism's adaptive capabilities is in its move-

ment from dependence on to transcendence of (an independence from) its sociality (refer to Figure 1, in "Introduction"). (For further discussion, refer to Mulkey, note 1, pp. 121–122.)

5. Quoted from Mulkey, p. 87.
6. The following section has been adapted from Mulkey, pp. 87–88.
7. Scholars debate the exact mechanisms of social behavior—producing and transmitting the rules of the group. Some, such as Talcott Parsons (see C. Camic, "Commentary," *American Sociological Review,* 55 [1990]: 313–345), contest the Watsonian behaviorist idea that recurrent human social behaviors (institutions) are the aggregate of individual attributes that derive from an assumption about the self-interested and rationally acting nature of the human and an evolution of progressively civilized (deference of self-gratification) behaviors that promote survival of members of the group. A theory of principles of sociology subsumes the Parsonian notion of values orientation by positing the determinateness in the kinds of cooperation valued by the group for its survival and ultimately forms of association (pattern variables) as expressive of the human evolution of self-interest to self-disinterest. (For further discussion, refer to Mulkey, note 2, p. 122.)
8. Peter Berger, *The Sacred Canopy: Elements of a Sociology Theory of Religion* (New York: Doubleday, 1967).
9. Reprinted with permission of the author.
10. Reprinted with permission of the author.
11. Reprinted with permission of the author.
12. Reprinted with permission of the author.
13. Emile Durkheim, *The Rules of Sociological Method* (New York: Free Press, 1964).
14. Karl Marx, *Capital: A Critique of Political Economy,* vol. 1 (New York: Random House, 1977; originally published in 1864).
15. Erving Goffman, *The Presentation of Self in Everyday Life* (Garden City, NY: Anchor, 1962).
16. George Herbert Mead, *Mind, Self and Society* (Chicago: University of Chicago Press, 1967).
17. Peter Berger, *Invitation to Sociology: A Humanistic Perspective* (New York: Doubleday, 1963).
18. The following section has been adapted from Mulkey, p. 88.
19. The following section has been adapted from Mulkey, pp. 89–91.
20. Jean Piaget, *The Construction of Reality in the Child* (New York: Basic Books, 1954) and *The Psychology of Intelligence* (London: Routledge and Kegan Paul, 1950).
21. Mead.
22. The following section has been adapted from Mulkey, pp. 91–93, 112–113.
23. Jean-Jacques Rousseau, *Émile,* trans. Allan Bloom (New York: Basic Books, 1979).

3

DOING WHAT OTHERS TELL US TO DO
Seeing Organization as Social Structure

◆ ARRANGEMENTS FOR SURVIVAL: THE GROUP

Between You and Me

Some Fathers Are Mothers

◆ FORMAL AND INFORMAL GROUPS

Telling the Grocery Store Cashier about Your Mother-in-Law

Separate Restrooms

*M*eet Dawn. She is society. In fact, Dawn is *family* as a set of instructions on how to feel and act toward others. The instructions are designated in her feelings and behaviors. She is not *in* a family; the family is in *her*.

For the whole entire fifteen years of my living in a stepparent family with my mother as the biological parent, I have not been able to get along with my stepfather. I have not been able to have any success-ful conversations with him either. Having this attitude toward my stepfather has created difficulties between my mother and me. She gets upset with me because he is her husband and I have no respect for him; I do not treat him as any type of parental figure.

After many years of very heartbreaking conflicts between my mother and myself, I continue to try to be civil with my stepfather. However, it is all an act. I do it for my mother's sake, to keep her happy. During the years of my growing up, my stepfather never interfered with my being scolded or with my punishments. Mostly, this was because my mother did not want him to. She would always say: "She is my daughter, and only I can tell her what to do." So if my stepfather ever did try to scold me in any way, my resentment for him increased drastically.

This resentment that I have, however, is what my question is. I do not know why I have this resentment. Is it because I was not happy about my parents' divorce? Is it because I was used to being with my mother alone for eight years, and then having this man come into our home? This topic has been something that has been bothering me for many years. I am trying to better understand my feelings toward my stepfather.[1]

We never think twice about why only certain persons live in houses together. Dawn's testimony shows how who she is aligns with the group. We restrict our arrangements with people so as to include a few and exclude others. For instance, only our biological fathers deserve our unconditional regard says society and so says Dawn.

Notice how Dawn refers to her stepfather as "this man" and that her behaviors and feelings for him are "resentment," "not respectful," "civil," and "an act." What has society said to Dawn to make her who she is and to make her have these feelings?

The fundamental instruction from society governing or determining Dawn as a personality is the *principle of organization*. This principle tells us how to arrange ourselves with others into groups to accomplish particular tasks as well as who and what to value in order to achieve goals defined by society. Children learn from society that they are supposed to have love, concern, and respect for only their biological parents. "He's my dad; I tell him things I never tell anyone else." A residential stepfather doesn't get this response.

I was on the crosstown bus recently, and a man in his thirties was making denigrating comments to the woman sitting next to him. It turned out that this person was his mother, yet he referred to her as "you bitch." The bus driver turned to him and yelled, "You better respect your mother, young man, or you will live a life of misery."

What is profound here is not that the bus driver heroically defended "poor Mom" but that society has achieved the remarkable accomplishment of getting us to feel and act toward amorphous protoplasm in the predictable ways known as "mother." My mother is enraged when I defy that an instinctual bond exists between us. I realize, though, that her feeling about so-called maternal instinct is analogous to the child in the pool who is afraid to swim, afraid of losing her known, familiar, and predictable repertoires for feeling and acting. The fact is, I know how to swim. I know that society makes provision for our cooperation with others in clear-cut ways. But these ways—even "mother" ways—are simply the means by which we, as humans, make cooperation possible. (Alice Rossi has shown that biological fathers can bond with infants equally as well as biological mothers.[2])

ARRANGEMENTS FOR SURVIVAL: THE GROUP

I say again, we know so little about ourselves. We act unaware of the determinants of our behavior, behavior that we feel is our own. We don't see the world. We see persons and things according to their social value.

Between You and Me

There can be nothing between you and me until we know what there should be between you and me. It's like two people confronting each other, each of whom speaks a language unknown to the other. Action bogs down. People don't know what to do in relation to each other; they cannot make known to each other their learned ways of feeling and acting. The most difficult lesson in sociology is to bring about the experience of what the Buddhists call the "beginner's mind." It's hard to believe that we can be aware of our being before we experience it as a judging being. When we are able to look at a sunset or a maggot crawling out of rotting flesh without judging one as beautiful and the other as ugly, we are reminded of our being. At moments like these, we can feel the excitement of *just being* without having to be on vacation, so to speak. To know yourself beyond social conditioning, wherever you are, is to make *being* a vacation.

We recurrently and without fail experience ourselves as the learned set of prescriptions that we have become. For example, in a classroom of students, people automatically will not sit in each others' laps, not because there is a sign posted forbidding this but because the sign is encoded in the mind, will, and emotion of each individual. Organizational rules dictate our behavior to the point where fish cannot talk about what it is like to be out of water; it's impossible. Dawn's disrespect for one person and not the other is socially styled, but to her, it's a natural response.

The principle of organization is that set of constraints imposed on human action such that people will act in predictable ways when they are with each other in groups. Sociologists say that for something to be a group, its members must view each other as members in an ongoing, enduring manner. People outside the group view members of the group as belonging to it or constituting it. Group members adopt a specific set of values ("goods" and "bads") and norms (expected behaviors that reflect the values).

So, a family is simply a set of society's instructions that have become the preferences and specific actions of the individuals in that group. Organizational rules for achieving the group—the family—tell who will be in the group: how many, what ages, what genders, what races and ethnicities, what religions, what educational levels. Organizational rules will tell us when and how much of our emotional, physical, and intellectual resources we will share with others in the group. The rules also tell us how long these relations are to last—a day or a lifetime.

Some Fathers Are Mothers

Now let's look at how the principle of organization creates the social phenomenon called *the group:* the family. Mothers are not maternal because they can biologically bear offspring. Some fathers are mothers by virtue of how they associate with members of the group. The arrangement of persons into this type of group requires instruction on what to value and how to reflect the value. The value of the unconditional regard is assigned to the status "mother." We need persons who are members of a group—family—who relate with and associate with others in the group with unconditional love. The value of unconditional acceptance means that a son can tell his mother "Ma, I'm on heroin," and her response will be "I love you anyway."

Members of this group recognize each other as family members—mother, father, son, and so on. They share a limited form of expression with other members of the group. A mother's regard for others in the group does not depend on how clean each keeps his teeth. Only Mom will love you under any circumstances. These associations are organized by society.

FORMAL AND INFORMAL GROUPS

Groups are provocative because we take them for granted. We conduct ourselves in and as the group. Our behavioral agendas are cast as a staggering variety of learned relations with others. Some of these relations are between two members; others are between two million. Some are secret; others are open. In some groups, members are closely knit and affectionate; in others, members are cold and indifferent.

Sociologists have not been very successful in neatly classifying groups. However, some commonly discussed groups are ingroups and outgroups, peer groups, reference groups, hierarchical triads, small and large groups, friendship groups, and primary and secondary groups (also referred to as *informal* and *formal* groups, respectively). Although these types of groups are those most often discussed, the analysis of *primary* and *secondary* groups will be very useful to our understanding of ourselves and society.

Telling the Grocery Store Cashier about Your Mother-in-Law

The distinction between formal and informal rules of organization amazingly empowers us to understand a great variety of human behaviors. The principles of sociology are actually all qualifications of the principle of organization. We never really consider why we think telling the grocery store cashier about our mother-in-law would be absurd. But our sociological analytical tool—the principle of organization—will adeptly provide us with the insight into why people act the ways they do.

Separate Restrooms

No one takes too much time to ponder why we have arranged ourselves so that men and women empty their bladders of bodily waste in separate rooms. Why indoors and in toilets? Why alone and in such privacy? Again, to understand what we falsely think is our individual behavior, we turn to the principle of organization.[3]

A primary group is any group in which social relationships, actual or expected, share the following characteristics; they are:

- Emotional—*interaction features the expression of affect or feelings such as joy or displeasure;*
- Diffuse—*the breadth of the interaction or its scope covers many aspects of life;*
- Particularistic—*the relationship is specific to the persons within the group (my friend, my father), not to a class of persons (clerks, police officers);*
- Collectivistic—*members are expected to guide their behavior based on what is good for the group overall;*
- Enduring—*members expect duration in their emotional commitments.*[4]

Members of primary groups are expected to feel and express emotion toward other members of their groups. The principle of organization is an incredible analytical device for understanding why we do what we do and not other things—why we act so concerted in our relations without questioning the felt naturalness of them. Primary groups reflect the conditioned ways in which we are expected to express a wide array of emotion, and every relationship we have is learned as the mind of the group. Each category of behaviors is imprinted on, as I say, our otherwise amorphous human protoplasm—a category called "father behaviors," "student behaviors," and so on. It's one thing to hug your father as a member of "the family" but another to hug your professor as a member of "the classroom." Members of a group of neurosurgeons in the operating room would not be interested in whether members of the group stop to hug their patients during surgical procedures.

The relations of members in a primary group are *diffuse*—individuals share many aspects of their experience. For example, expectations for members of the group "the classroom" are learned and become part of each individual's cognition, emotion, and behavior according to a set of directions labeled "student." Thus, in the group "the classroom," telling the student sitting next to you that you have diarrhea because you put too many prunes in your cereal for breakfast is an aspect of experience not considered appropriate for members of that group. Under these conditions, the group cannot accomplish its tasks.

The relations of primary-group members are also *particularistic;* the obligations of persons to each other are specific to only one member of the group, in general. As a member of the group "the family," I feel right in paying for my daughter's college education but not my neighbor's daughter's education.

The relations of persons who are members of a primary group are *collectivistic,* so that each individual's behavior is in the interests of everybody in the group. A family member, for example, would take a portion of a bowl of rice prepared for a family meal, not all of it.

When the principle of organization directs the feelings and actions of members of primary groups, those people expect their relatedness to *endure.* A person organized emotionally, cognitively, and behaviorally as a "parent" and belonging to the group "the family" is committed to his offspring for a lifetime, whereas the commitment of a waitress to a client is short lived.

Formally organized relationships differ from the relationships that constitute primary groups. Such *secondary groups* are:

- *Emotionally neutral;*
- *Segmented, or narrow;*
- *Universalistic;*
- *Self-interested;*
- *Not enduring.*[5]

Persons are organized by society (others) to participate as members of secondary groups. This set of relations is noticeably void of emotion. To be "male," for example, is to belong to an aggregate, or group, in which members are generally taught in their relations to others not to emote. Members of the group "females," however, are taught to emote. These patterns are reflected in the hiring practices of certain occupations, such as science and engineering, where males are, on average, recruited more often; given the organization of the male personality, it is believed that males will not let emotion interfere with performing a task. People organized in personality to be more emotional—females—will supposedly be distracted and unable to perform the technical procedures required for these types of jobs.

Persons formally organized as members of various groups relate restricted features of their experience. I would be startled if a member of the group "piano tuners," while on call at my home, finished tuning the piano and proceeded to pull out from her bag a pair of pajamas, change into them, and crawl into bed in one of the rooms in my house. Sleeping on the job is not a behavior considered acceptable in the relation between the piano tuner and the client.

Be sure to note how automatically you would be properly shocked if a student in your class reached into your book bag, found your wallet, and took a few dollars. For social creatures, every behavior is socially structured, but the reality of this is not readily available in our awareness. Members that make up formally organized groups share very limited behaviors with others.

When persons are organized to interact formally, they are universalistic in their relations. All members of the group are treated alike. All students, for instance, are graded by the same standards. Members express formal organization when their behaviors are not in the interests of everyone but are self-interested. A family member acts formally when he seeks a divorce from his present spouse to marry a person with higher income, despite the negative effects that breaching the marriage obligations has on the child members of the group.

The formal relations of secondary groups are exemplified by indefinite commitment in relating to other members of the group. Because formal organizations of persons are universalistic in contrast to particularistic and individualistic in contrast to collectivistic, the relations of the group continue or dissolve. Mulkey's Introduction to Sociology class continues with the different students who comprise it from semester to semester, but when members of a family leave, the family does not continue.

We have now seen social structure in the case of the principle of organization: rules for arranging ourselves into groups to accomplish tasks. Just when we imagine we are unique individuals and believe we personally have our lives under control, along comes the sociologist and says, "No, we don't." The illusion is that things seem under control because they have already been decided.

Society makes people respond according to rules for informal arrangements. In informal arrangements, the responses are more emotional, diffuse, particularistic, collectivistic, and enduring than the emotionally neutral, narrow, universalistic, self-interested, and nonenduring responses dictated by formal organization rules. That is why Dawn doesn't respect her stepfather. It's not that he's proven himself to be a lousy guy, but society says that any stepfather is a lousy guy and that only a biological father deserves his offspring's emotional commitment.

As does every chapter in this book, this chapter ends by pointing to the essential insights of sociology. First, we see social structure. We come to realize that personality belongs to society. The principle of organization constitutes much (if not all) of the personal and predictable set of emotions and orientations to others and our world—Dawn's to her stepfather, for instance. Sociology's first essential insight allows us to see who we think we are, so that inevitably we ask, Who are we really?

Sociology's second essential insight is itself. Sociology—itself an understanding, a consciousness of the social self—is the very object for transcendence. It provides the occasion for moving on in our self-development. It represents many bruised, scabbed, and scarred knees from the movement from crawling to walking in our development as humans. Our attachment to or identity with our social nature makes our lives a certain way. When we know ourselves solely as society, then we are constantly up and down emotionally, defending what we experience or know as ourselves in the way that society organizes. By seeing that "stepfather" is just a learned way of relating to a human being, Dawn is less determined or affected by her feelings of disrespect; she observes them and dismisses them or acts on them with ease. In seeing, we can become sensitive to the self that is not society or in society but that society is in!

GLOSSARY

collectivistic relations Interactional rules for informal organization that specify behavior that is good for the group overall. For example, you will help your sister because she is part of your family; you wouldn't help just any person.

diffuse relations Interactional rules for informal organization that specify the cultivation and expression of a broad scope of the personality. It is expected, for example, that you share with other members of your family everything that happens in the day, but you wouldn't share these things with the cashier in the market.

emotional relations Interactional rules for informal organization that specify the cultivation and expression of emotion. For example, humans who are biologically female become socially female by learning that, in many situations, expressing emotion as crying is okay; the social category "male," however, includes instructions that tell men not to emote, especially not to cry.

enduring relations Interactional rules for informal relations that specify duration in emotional commitment to others. The family, for instance, exists until "death us do part," so to speak. The group of shoppers at Macy's, however, does not depend on any commitment for it to continue.

formal organization One of two main types of arrangements with others; characterized by segmented, emotionally neutral, universalistic, self-interested, and nonenduring relations.

informal organization One of two main types of arrangements with others; characterized by diffuse, emotional, particularistic, collectivistic, and enduring relations.

nonemotional relations Interactional rules for formal organization that specify not to react emotionally to a person, thing, or situation (that is, to withhold emotion). For example, we learn not to feel emotion toward the student next to us in class in the way we would feel toward a sibling.

organization, principle of A guideline for arranging ourselves with others into groups for accomplishing given tasks.

particularistic relations Interactional rules for informal organization that specify that our relations with others are unique to the individual. For example, I treat all students alike when I grade them on the same basis, but when I call each by his first name, I am relating to him for a unique quality. Likewise, we don't treat all spouses and children alike, only our spouse and our children.

primary group See *informal organization.*

secondary group See *formal organization.*

segmented relations Interactional rules for formal organization that specify the development and expression of a narrow range of personality. For example, you talk to the shoe salesperson only about purchasing shoes, not about your headache.

universalistic relations Interactional rules for formal organization that specify that people are to be treated alike. For example, I grade all students on the same basis.

NOTES

1. Reprinted with permission of the author.
2. Alice Rossi, "Gender and Parenthood," *American Sociological Review*, 161 (February 1984): 189.
3. The following discussion of groups has been adapted from Lynn M. Mulkey, *Sociology of Education: Theoretical and Empirical Investigations* (Orlando, FL: Harcourt Brace Jovanovich, 1993), pp. 166–168. The discussion is founded on the insights of two established sociologists: Robert K. Merton and William J. Goode. For a more thorough analysis, see the following: Merton, "The Classification of Types of Membership Groups," in *Social Theory and Social Structure*, enlarged ed. (New York: Free Press, 1968), pp. 362–380, and Goode, "Forms of Social Organization: Groups Large and Small," in *Principles of Sociology* (New York: McGraw-Hill, 1977), pp. 174–207.
4. Quoted from Mulkey, pp. 166–167. Goode (see note 3) uses the descriptive concepts (called *pattern variables*) of Talcott Parsons, except for the final one: *enduring*. According to Goode, his fifth concept is *ascriptive–achieved*, but in primary relations, no specification requires that the relation be one or the other. For a discussion of these ideas, Goode recommends consulting Parsons, *The Social System* (New York: Free Press, 1951), pp. 55–88. The terms elaborate on the concepts "gemeinschaft" and "gesellschaft," which are discussed in the last part of the chapter on forms of social organization.
5. Quoted from Mulkey, p. 168.

4

DOING WHAT OTHERS TELL US TO DO
Seeing Institutions as Social Structure

◆ SOCIETY: DICTATES OF THE BIG GROUP

Meet My Mother: Society

Understanding the Ocean, the Symphony, and Society
by Looking at the Fish, the Musician, and You

◆ INSTITUTIONS: LARGE-SCALE, MACRODETERMINANTS OF
WHAT WE DO

Learning to Use a Fork, a Credit Card, and College Credentials

Personality in Society versus Society in Personality

*M*eet Murray. He is not who you might think he is, and, more importantly, he is not who he thinks he is. He is not an individual as much as he is society. To understand him, you must know something about society.

Fundamentally, Murray is amorphous protoplasm. Society embodies itself as his personality—the consolidation of the group's instructions about how he should feel and act toward things and toward others in the world. Some instructions are called "student" instructions. Murray is aware of these instructions only as himself. He perceives his feelings and actions as inherent, natural, belonging to him. But Murray first belongs to society, and we understand him when we understand society.

The understanding of ourselves as society has a peculiar relevance for our being in the world. For Murray, these new perceptions make him either anxiously dependent on his school achievement for his psychological and existential well-being or peaceful, anchored, and stable in a self that recognizes it never belonged to him in the first place. Ironically, in this recognition, Murray is better at getting good grades.

Having been a valedictorian in all three of my previous schools, elementary, junior high, and high school, I have often wondered what it is that propels me to frantically achieve academically. Since the beginning of my academic career, way back in elementary school, I can recall students around me approaching school and the responsibilities that come with it with a relative nonchalance while I would be diligently preparing for my next assignment or exam.

As I look back at these earlier days, now a more mature, educated young man, I feel that, more than anything else, the relentless inspiration I received from my parents accounted for these differences. For as long as I can remember, my parents, particularly my mother, pushed me almost obsessively to do well, assuring me that, with the right education and educational goals, all the things prerequisite to a happy, fulfilling life could be mine. The big extravagant home in an exclusive neighborhood, the prestigious car, the means to more than adequately support a wife and children are all things I have been taught hinge upon just how far I wish to go in my studies and my performance in them.

Don't parents, in fact, have a significant influence over our educational goals and will to achieve? By the time we begin our early schooling, our parents have already begun to transmit to us the rules of the society that if we work our hardest in school to achieve our potential and set high educational goals for ourselves, all the desirable things in life can be ours. I internalized these rules, and the "need" to achieve the grade and later the educational goal became an intricate part of myself. Depending on the success of this socialization, I may become dominated by this social self and view any setbacks to these social obligations as a loss of my identity. This is in me when I'm afraid to share with my parents a bad grade or, in a more extreme instance, in me when I feel incapable of living up to the expectations of society.[1]

Amazingly, society's need to prepare people with the kinds of skills and knowledge to sustain itself is reflected in the rules transmitted to Murray and internalized as his personality. What is intimately Murray's felt need for achievement is actually society's general prescription. Maybe Murray acknowledges that his parents were instrumental in developing his preference for achievement by rewarding him for good school performance. But what is seemingly personal as the individual's is really universal and impersonal as the group's. We must ask, in this case (as in all cases), If Murray is society, then what is individual about him? Once we are able to see society as Murray, we can unsee society and understand what it means to be an individual.

*I*t's one thing to realize that you learned from your parents to love eating scallops instead of squirrel, but it's another thing to realize that what seems private, personal, and, again, very much your own, really belongs to something as impersonal as society, the general and more universal body of rules. We don't fathom or fully comprehend that without society's imposition of ordering our actions toward others, we are literally at a loss of what to do with ourselves. We are perhaps worse off than other organisms that are instinctively, automatically related in their responses to things. Humans, without a social program, are without themselves. We cannot even give our attention long enough to any aspect of experience and know what to do, what to feel, what it is in relation to the world.

SOCIETY: DICTATES OF THE BIG GROUP

Sociologists contribute to our self-understanding by showing us that the self, for the most part (at least the first part but not the final part) *is* the group. Students may not always obey their teachers (or their parents), but they actually obey another teacher—society, with its expectations for formal learning. In some human societies, survival has depended more on the ability of the young male members to master hunting skills than on achieving high scores on graduate-school admissions examinations. *Education* is just a name for a set of human relations that society has decided are important.

Meet My Mother: Society

All along, it has felt like we were being obedient to Mom and getting her approval, her affirmation of our worth in the world. But Mom, says sociology, is society's designation, an assignment of relatedness, for how to satisfy biological needs. For example, if our social arrangements did not get us food, we would die; if they did not make us care for the young, our offspring would die. However, the kinds of social organization designed to meet these biological imperatives vary greatly, except at what appears to be a basic level of determinateness. Biology ensures the recurrence of social arrangements that make life possible.

The biological foundations necessary to be social are the principles of sociology, which predispose us to act socially (that is, to make and to follow prescriptions for behavior) in six primary ways. At the individual level, the principle of institutions is the predisposition to make shared rules that result in provisions for childrearing, distributing scarce resources, and so on. When these rules become collective, they are the externalized form of individual subjective consciousness; ultimately, the rules take on objective existence as society. Society is first to dictate how we should behave, and in this way, we are rule following before we are rule making.

Another way to think about the principle of institutions is that it is an elaboration of the principle of organization, where no one individual but society at large arranges individuals in personality into groups to accomplish its goals. The values and norms that we embody reflect categories of behaviors—statuses and roles as they constitute a whole interrelated system of relationships.

Understanding the Ocean, the Symphony, and Society by Looking at the Fish, the Musician, and You

To make sense of why Murray says what he does, we will think of him as what a fish is to an ocean or what a musician is to an orchestra. We understand what a fin is when we know the organism inhabits the ocean; we understand the musical note when we hear the whole symphony. We understand Murray when we know he represents one small part of concerted human relations.

The *principle of institutions* is a composite of all the principles of social life, clusters of ordered behavior that accomplish the satisfaction of general human needs.[2] Society is a system comprised of subsystems that ensure the following relations:

1. Reproduction of members of the society and nurturing the young (the family)
2. Distribution of resources (the economy)
3. Protection from internal and external threats (the military and police)
4. Selection and allocation of persons to occupations (education)
5. Conformity to the system's expectations of behavior by defining an ultimate purpose to the unknown (religion)

Each institution contributes to a total set of social relations that sustain human survival.[3] Recall from Chapter 1 that any social phenomenon (or way in which other people influence our behavior through constraints on how we think, feel, and act) has a *systemic* property. The rules for behavior have a structure, or interrelatedness, to a whole set of behaviors. The musician's part can be understood in light of the sound of the whole musical score. A person's individual behavior is part of the whole, but the whole cannot be found in one individual. Murray's behavior can be understood only in the context of the whole society, not just in his relations with his mother or his teacher. Murray's mother is a set of relations that are part of a cluster of defined behaviors that constitute family relatedness. "The family" is a constellation of categories of behaviors prescribed to humans, so that when persons relate according to "mother" rules or "son" rules, they are manifesting the group "the family." "Mother" rules guarantee that Murray will be nurtured. "Mother" is nothing more than society's prescription for what to do in relation to another human being to accomplish a valued outcome.

To understand Murray's very intimate feeling, his drive to achieve, we can turn to the principle of institutions. The principles of sociology operate together in a particular configuration as the principle of institutions; thus, we can interpret Murray's behavior both *microscopically* and *macroscopically*. The importance Murray assigns to grades belongs to him at the microscopic level, but first, at the macroscopic level, it belongs to society. Think of the rules as cells comprising organs and the organs as comprising whole living systems. What goes on as Murray's feelings and actions (the cellular level) is ordered according to sets of rules (organs). That is, what goes on between the institution of education and the institutions of the family, religion, and government are found as Murray's behavior. Society represents itself in Murray as the whole symphony does in the musician—as a particular value and set of behaviors.

Interinstitutionally, the principle of institutions operates as education in relation to other institutions and between institutions (across societies). At an even greater level of abstraction, each society is part of a global system, and we can think of this system as the macrodeterminant of Murray's behavior. Compare this systemic feature of social phenomena—the interconnections of macro- and microlevel explanations of our behavior—with how a capitalistic economic institution is a set of relations that are justified by a religious institution that fosters a belief in unregulated enterprise, an educational institution that encourages competition. A system with a socialist economy would have institutional interrelations that intercorrelate.

Perhaps this is the repeated message in this book's introduction to introductions of sociology: As a sociologist, you can come to see that people have, in a sense, been deceived in claiming our actions as our own. That analytical concept, the principle of institutions, makes available to us, rather dramatically, a vision of how an individual, such as Murray, represents the group. The felt proprietorship, the sense that this is *me*, individually, is actually part of a stable cluster of values—norms arranged into categories called *statuses* and *roles* that ultimately make recognizable the relations of persons in groups. Society needs members who want good grades. Society tells Murray to feel and act according to a category of behaviors that society needs—"student." Murray's thoughts and actions are determined by society to solve the problem of living with others. As a learned set of relations ("student" relations), Murray comes to value intellectual pursuit; he acts this out with others by going to school.

Some sociologists view the recurrent relations manifesting the rules of institutions from a *functionalist* perspective, where the major function of education is as a set of relations that play an important part in maintaining the equilibrium of the whole system. Any society that fails to inculcate in its new members the rules of the group will break down. *Conflict* theorists explain that the principle of institutions is a relationship that benefits some members of society more than others. The relative explanatory power of these theories is not discussed here.[4]

INSTITUTIONS: LARGE-SCALE, MACRODETERMINANTS OF WHAT WE DO

Sociology's essential insights make us turn to society as the cause of Murray's behavior and ask us to consider, Just who is Murray? Is he a mere replication, a rubber stamp of society? Think about it this way:

Clusters of values and norms designed to establish recurrent features of thought and action to meet social demands are the family, religion, economy/polity, medicine, and sports. The family organizes us to care for our biological offspring and to want sexual relations with a limited number of persons. Religion grounds human values and norms in a belief system. The economic and political systems regulate the production and distribution of goods and services and maintain order. Medicine makes provision for people who are sick. The family needs persons to relate, such as "mothers," but Mother is not aware that her feeling of pride over having a child is society's pride. By identifying with or being aware of herself as a mother, she is really and fundamentally a person who, under society's sponsorship, feels and acts in ways we assign according to a category of rules called "mother." In other words, society tells her to take physical attributes into consideration—the childbearing capability—and to consider it important, overlook it, or do this or that with it.

Some sociologists have tried to explain changes in institutions according to the ecological environment in which a society exists.[5] Societies must develop human relations as subsistence strategies (such as hunting and gathering, agriculture, industry). For example, take the case of a land where there is a limited water supply. For survival of the group, society would organize its members to conserve and provide a surplus of water. Through the relations known as family, society would ensure that children who are biologically predisposed to sweating when they get emotional would learn not to emote and thus not to sweat. Persons with a biological predisposition not to sweat profusely when being emotional would be encouraged to express emotion. Instead of statuses that include only child and parent, the family would have the "sweats" and the "non-sweats" in order to fulfill society's architecture for survival.

Learning to Use a Fork, a Credit Card, and College Credentials

In attempting to understand Murray's behavior, think about how observing a person who eats mashed potatoes with her fingers, who pays for everything in cash as opposed to credit, or who doesn't have a college degree evokes from your sentiment and mine feelings of disrespect. Why are my feelings about this person not mine as much as they are society's? Why is that which is seemingly and again so personally mine under the auspices of something very remote from my immediate awareness? Why is Murray's need to achieve above all society's need? More astonishingly, there is not one human orientation that is not in some way a representation of society!

A sociological analysis always entails the application of the principles of sociology to human action, the biological predispositions to making rules for living cooperatively. These principles work simultaneously to bring about coordinated human activity. To understand Murray's behavior, we must understand that education—the principle of institutions that constrains human behavior to accomplish the transmission of a society's knowledge and skills to each generation—includes the operation of the principle of socialization. Through socialization, individuals acquire their preferences. The value on intelligence is inculcated, as are norms such as mandatory school attendance according to the statuses of "teacher" and "student."

So, in this chapter, we have applied sociology's essential insights in a useful way to make sense of Murray's behavior. We have examined education sociologically by applying one of the major analytical conceptual tools of the field: the principle of institutions. Most fundamentally, education is an institution, the collective representation of the human predisposition to follow group rules by making provisions that sustain the well-being of the group and each member. In this case, education, as an institution, is viewed as expectations that guide the development of individuals to fit into the society, especially into occupational roles.

Insight into Murray, using the principle of institutions, is gleaned by observing this principle from several perspectives, as it operates as part of a global system of societies. In this light, the principle is seen as interdependent with education across societies in its function in a global system. Further understanding of the characteristic operation of the principle of institutions is obtained by viewing education within U.S. society, in relation to other institutions, and by viewing education globally, in relation to other educational systems. From our investigation, the principle of institutions tells us what it means to be *educated* and why Murray wants good grades. Evidence supports those who argue that the institution of education represents the collective agreements to prepare persons in relation to the economic development aims of the system; elements of both coercion and consensus are attributes of the principle's operation.

What is clear from our sociological understanding of institutions—and particularly of education as a set of relations—is the predominance of the patterned and functionally integrative nature of behavioral prescriptions toward global, societal, and individual levels of cooperation. Amazingly, the global rules are in Murray as his personality.

Personality in Society versus Society in Personality

We return now to the idea of sociology's essential insights. By helping us see who we thought we were—a social self—we can remain in society, where personality is (in) society and society is a dependence. Or we can develop from this dependence on society to independence, and society will then be in personality. The a priori self is what matters. *Seeing* is what is miraculous, not *what* you see. We can use a fork, a credit card, and college credentials, but it's the fact that we can do these things, not the things themselves, that matters in the perception of who we are. Murray is valedictorian, Murray is society, and then Murray is that which is able to be society.

GLOSSARY

economy/polity Institutions that regulate the production and distribution of goods and services and maintain order.

education An institution that organizes to transmit the values and norms of society. Education promotes the mastery of knowledge and skills necessary for fulfilling allocated occupations.

family An institution that regulates sexual behavior and guarantees the care of children.

institutions, principle of The principle of organization at the macro-level (arrangement of individuals into a large group or society to accomplish survival); the rules of the group, or social structure, statuses, roles and their accompanying values, and norms as they are part of a large, interrelated system designed to promote the well-being of each member.

religion An institution that promotes social solidarity by grounding values and norms in belief.

NOTES

1. Reprinted with permission of the author.
2. This section is based on Lynn M. Mulkey, *Sociology of Education: Theoretical and Empirical Investigations* (Orlando, FL: Harcourt Brace Jovanovich, 1993), pp. 68–70.
3. Sociologists often study other institutions (such as sports, science, etc.) that are not discussed here.
4. Theories explain the nature of principles, particularly as to their stratification characteristics. Therefore, the principle of stratification operates in conjunction with all other principles and is evidenced in discussion of the theoretical interpretation of the natures of other principles. See Randall Collins, "Functional and Conflict Theories of Educational Stratification," *American Sociological Review*, 36, no. 6 (1971): 1002–1019. Also see Samuel Bowles and Herbert Gintis, *Schooling in Capitalist America: Educational Reform and the Contradictions of Economic Life* (New York: Basic Books, 1976). See also this book, Chapter 2, note 7.
5. See Talcott Parsons, *Societies: Evolutionary and Comparative Perspectives* (Englewood Cliffs, NJ: Prentice Hall, 1966).

5

WHAT WE WANT
AND WHAT WE GET
Seeing Stratification as
Social Structure

◆ ALLOCATING WEALTH, POWER, AND PRESTIGE

Being Japanese, Preferring Calculus to Pizza, and
Becoming an Engineer

Dependency, the Law, and Living and Dying by the Sword

Nobody Said It Would Be Easy

◆ ARE SOME PEOPLE WORTH MORE THAN OTHERS?

Self-Defense: Fiercely Bravado in My Cotton Tee

Prince: "Everything You Do Is Success"

Sociotherapy: Breaking Down Defenses

*M*eet Theresa. She is society. Society has allocated how it will distribute the desirable things in life (wealth, power, and prestige) as her.

I have been bulimic in the past and still am occasionally. I have cut out purging mostly, but I still have a compulsion to eat. It is a constant struggle every day to eat only when I am hungry.

I think that I started to diet because most women I knew as an adolescent, including my mother, were always on diets. It seemed like the thing to do; it seemed like all women did it. In one way, I remember that I thought it would be fun to do, and in another way, I thought I was supposed to do it.

I really have a problem with an eating disorder now. My eating patterns often prevent me from participating in the normal activities of everyday life. If I eat anything when I am not hungry (even if it is one tiny thing), I automatically feel very depressed because I feel like I have failed at something. I don't know what I have to do to get out of this terrible cycle.

Only recently have I thought about eating disorders as caused by society's dictation of the thin ideal. I always attributed my problem to my own personality and the eating patterns I learned from home. I am now realizing that the patterns I learned at home came from a greater source: society. If there was not such a great emphasis placed on thinness, then I probably never would have dieted at all. I also probably would not think I was such a terrible person if I was not equal to the thin ideal that society dictates to me.

Society tells me how to feel better or worse about certain characteristics, whether ascribed or achieved. It ranks people according to these characteristics, and they are rewarded accordingly. Society tells us that, to have wealth, we must have money, property, or beauty, and society defines beauty as the thin ideal. When society tells us what beauty is, we assume they are correct, and we feel like outcasts if we do not conform to society's expectations. Models, for example, have prestige and are paid highly simply because of their beauty.

I chose to review a study where the hypothesis tested is that depression and eating disorders in women are due to the thin ideal that society forces on women. This study attempts to explain why twice as many women as men are likely to be depressed, why this sex difference starts at puberty, why this sex difference is only found in Western countries, why there is more depression today, and why the average age of the onset for depression is younger than ever. The study attempts to explain why four of these trends are parallel to trends in eating disorders. The majority of eating disorder patients are female, eating disorders emerge at puberty, eating disorders are present in Western cultures and absent in non-Western cultures, and eating disorders have increased over the past 20 years.[1]

Next, meet Ayanna. She is also society. As with Theresa, society has allocated how it will distribute the desirable things in life (wealth, power, and prestige) as Ayanna. In her case, Ayanna feels that she is less important than other people because of the color of her skin: Black. Society dictates what attributes we should attend to and then how. We act toward others according to how we have learned to feel about them—specifically, in terms of their ascriptive (arbitrary, something a person cannot change) or meritocratic (achieved, something a person can work for) value. A person cannot achieve another skin color, so she cannot achieve more of society's rewards.

On occasion, over the past several years of my adult life, I've often wondered why my glancing upon a Black male–White female couple has irritated me so. What I've discovered is that I am chagrined when I've observed a somewhat good-looking, astute, prosperous, highly visible Black male comfortably positioned in the company of a White female. My most recent encounter with this feeling was after viewing a televised basketball game, and one of the Black team players' wives was introduced at the intermission, and to much of my surprise, she was White. . . .

The ambiance that overcomes me during such episodes is not just a repulsive feeling toward the men but my feeling of "Black women, you don't rate, you don't qualify, this limelight is not for you." I have often found myself coveting my White counterpart. I feel emotional torture when I compare myself with the White woman wrapped around a Black male, and I ask myself, Why her and not someone of his own race? Is the harsh reality that White women rate more than Black women?

In my search for understanding this experience, I am learning the answer lies within the construct of society; it governs my emotions. My expectations and disappointments have been ordered by some mechanism or principle of society that I intend to unravel for my own sanity. Why does society dictate to a Black woman that she is not worthy of the rewards a highly visible Black man can give her?

The sociological principle associated with this study is stratification. This principle includes the process of assigning social value to various attributes of an individual whereby the individual and the group come to view themselves and act as worthy or unworthy recipients of reward. Sometimes you can change your value, and sometimes you cannot. According to the research study I reviewed ("Marketplace Economy: The Evaluation of Interracial Couples," Basic and Applied Psychology, *1991), Elder's marketplace concept of stratification—of how people are assigned a value—females use attractiveness to buy the best mates (i.e., high-status husbands), while males use socioeconomic status to buy attractive wives. In Porterfield's status incongruity concept, White females who marry Black males are perceived as lowering themselves or marrying below their social class, regardless of their level of physical attractiveness. Stratification operates so that positive evaluation depends on "equitable exchange" of persons' valued attributes. The stratification principle has explained the insecurities I have experienced.*[2]

What's better, what's worse, what's mine, what's yours are social instructions. As I was walking home the other night and peered into the window of the house on the corner of the street where I live, I became aware of a feeling that I typically never question: I felt that the house *belonged* to them, not to me. I therefore would never consider walking into the house uninvited and sitting down on the couch in the living room.

Belonging is fundamentally another of society's instructions for behavior that promotes my survival in the group. Of course, that sounds purely intellectual, but practically and radically speaking, belonging is reduced to that very feeling and behavior that I claim as mine. *Mine* is society's. The feeling that *this* belongs to me and *that* to them is socially contrived. Now let's examine how our feelings become ordered by society.

ALLOCATING WEALTH, POWER, AND PRESTIGE

It's one thing to *say* that society designates under what conditions we acquire the desirable things in life, but it's another thing to *feel* it as me. Society confers upon me, for example, my embarrassment when I am naked in the pool shower room alongside one of my students who is showering. I am embarrassed because only people of the same supposed value in society can share their nakedness. That is, as a professor, my status allows me to protect my nakedness as a private domain, not to be trespassed on by persons of lower status.

Theresa feels society as her need to be thin. She is supposed to be thin to be considered an attractive woman. Ayanna feels society as her oppression as a Black woman. She feels inferior and undeserving, particularly in comparison to White women.

Every human group needs to solve the problem of who gets what and under what conditions; otherwise, I would feel no discomfort, emotionally, in walking into just anybody's house uninvited.[3] Theresa's feeling that she will be valued under the terms of thinness—and how much and in what ways—reflects the *principle of stratification* in operation. These rules govern who is worthy and who is not worthy of what rewards (wealth, power, and prestige), how they will be allocated (on what basis), and how they become manifested as the emotional and behavioral characteristics of persons.

Human relations depend on how we learn to pay attention to things, how to value some things and not others, and how much and when. This is the general mechanism of stratification; it is the stratification of our judgment of things. Stratification as rule making makes us feel that some things are worth paying attention to and others are not, and it contributes simultaneously (alongside and inextricably in conjunction) with the other principles that constitute human rule making. The principle of stratification, theoretically, has a relative tendency to operate on the basis of conflict and/or consensus, that is, coercively, serving the interests of a few, or democratically, representing the interests of many.

Being Japanese, Preferring Calculus to Pizza, and Becoming an Engineer

Why is it that Asian students are, on the average, better in calculus than students from other racial and ethnic groups? Why might they prefer to spend their time doing mathematics homework rather than eating pizza with friends? Why also do math-related and scientific jobs tend to recruit Asian students?

People vary in what they want, in what they get, and in getting what they want.[4] Sociologists speculate as to whether everyone can have equal material and emotional rewards and how different rewards accompany different attributes in a society.[5] For example, occupations are valued in similar ways across societies. The value of a job depends on how valuable it is and how many persons are available to fill it. Now, beyond this intellectual assertion, find in your own self-judgment your self-evaluation based on what kind of job you want or have. For women, work has been unpaid and in the home, and Theresa's attributes of "female," and "thin" signify the ascriptive way in which society awards her personhood.

The strata that are comprised of persons with valued attributes are based on three dimensions—*wealth, power,* and *prestige*—sometimes referred to as *social class.*[6] Sociologists use the term *socioeconomic status (SES),* an index based on three measures or indicators of rewards (income, type of occupation, and years of education), to note a person's social worth.

The rules for who gets what and under what conditions also involve whether the boundaries between the strata are fixed or permeable. An *ascribed status* is one characteristic of a *closed* social system, where rewards are assigned to individuals on a basis other than their earning them through merit. Membership is based on an assigned quality, such as skin color, gender, freckles, or pimples. An *achieved status* allows persons to change the condition of their rewards through merit or achievement; these are the conditions of an *open* stratification system. Moving from one status to another is referred to as *social mobility,* where a person can change his life chances from one generation to the next by becoming a lawyer if his father was a plumber. This change in rewards or social mobility also relies on *exchange* and *structural* features of the group. When persons in highly rewarded jobs lose those jobs and those in the less-rewarded jobs are promoted, this is *exchange mobility*. When changes in the types of jobs needed make available new positions, we observe *structural mobility*.

Successful people are those who have the right characteristics, ascribed and achieved. For example, the well-paid corporate manager might be valued for being White, male, educated, and hard working. He embodies society's values and is rewarded for both wanting to do calculus and actually doing it instead of for loving it but working at a pizza shop.

Dependency, the Law, and Living and Dying by the Sword

We get to know society by getting to know ourselves. Whenever we feel better than another person or want something he has, it's because the rules for getting and having have become our very personality. What's even more interesting is that we judge ourselves by society's standards. We feel ecstatic if we meet its standards and depressed if we don't. Society, you see, is us.

That is what drives Theresa to bulimia. We are all like her in that we depend on society to tell us who we are and how well we are doing at being society. In our personality, we are consciously aware of all of those views of ourselves that society values. When we are unable to be what society says we should be, we feel less like selves. Not only do we get ourselves from society but we defend the definitions of ourselves that society provides. If society says that it values women for having children, then if a woman doesn't have a child, she doesn't feel like a person, a self. I have many female friends who have reached the end of their childbearing years and feel that they are not persons because they haven't had children.

Nobody Said It Would Be Easy

I marvel sometimes—in fact, many times—at how, as a research consultant for the New York City Public Schools, I have learned that the biggest determinant of how well a child will do in school is whether he is from a poor household. Poverty predicts life chances. A child's access to wealth, power, and prestige has less to do with his abilities and more to do with his family background. I've also learned that Americans say that the rules for getting the desirable things in life must be fair. But the child of the ghetto typically tells himself that he might as well give up, since he will never be what society expects, or he might even try to achieve success but fail. Nobody said it would be easy, but perhaps only the child who can distinguish his value beyond social value and is taught that he is not society will have enough faith in himself to deviate from what society says he should be.

ARE SOME PEOPLE WORTH MORE THAN OTHERS?

Why do some people have more of the desirable things in life than others? Do the differences alone matter, or is it how the differences are valued? Does this mean that some people are better than others?

Many people in the United States believe in differences, in inequality, but they believe that the rules for obtaining society's rewards must be fair. Some people, for example, are rewarded simply on the basis of appearance—perhaps for their breast size. We sort persons or give attention to them on the basis of their genitals. Those having female genitals have the status "woman" and are given attention associated with (rewarded for) being sexual objects. "Here I am: breasts. Think about me and relate to me as sexual." Society encourages women to seek rewards for being sexual, bearing children, and being nurturing, but the rewards for these attributes are less than those for other characteristics, such as cognitive facility. (And in women, cognitive facility is given less attention than in men.) Other people are rewarded because they have worked hard to get where they are—for instance, the ballerina who practices four hours per day, routinely.

We, as society, sort people on the basis of characteristics and then rank them in a hierarchy, from top to bottom. This hierarchy represents society's structure and includes a dimension of constraint in the name of cooperation: People who have various amounts of scarce but desirable resources or rewards form layers, or *strata* (hence the term *stratification*).

Also noteworthy (and true for all of the social principles that operate on us, not only stratification) is the degree to which stratification is ingrained as part of the social programming of individuals. Consider how little we think about stratification, despite its profound influence. We react to prescriptions of stratification in the same way we respond to gravity: matter of factly. Unfortunately, this response brings with it the consequence that we come to experience inequality and to perceive ourselves as better or worse (selves) than others, based on our position in the social strata. We have difficulty (until, of course, we study sociology) in sensing ourselves as valuable apart from our learned way to judge ourselves, others, and the world.

Self-Defense: Fiercely Bravado in My Cotton Tee

Cotton t-shirts are "in" these days; they symbolize a daring lifestyle, taking chances, and the like. But more importantly, cotton t-shirts are *in* us, not *on* us. We don't notice that we feel good when we wear something that's "in." Not only that, we judge ourselves and others if we or they are not "in." We might get upset and defend ourselves if someone insults us for not wearing a cotton t-shirt, or we might limit our relations to those who wear cotton tees. We might even feel more valuable as persons compared to those who don't wear cotton tees, and we might even chop off people's heads in the name of cotton t-shirts because we think they are us (just like we think our gender, our age, our race, or the number of hairs in our eyebrows is us). Why?

Sociology tells us that society is not beside us or on us but in us. Society thinks as us, acts as us, is us. But as we will see in later chapters, this way of experiencing ourselves as selves is only one way and is a necessary step in developing a second way of experiencing ourselves as selves. We constantly monitor the self-awareness that society gives to us. As I board the train, I judge every head that comes in the door: This one has oily hair, this one has no hair, this one has too much hair, too much makeup, too much jewelry, a great jacket, too many blackheads. Or at the swimming pool, girls chatter in the locker room, "He's so ugly," "You're so fat," "He's wasted," "You've got a great body."

Our minds, our emotions, our actions are not really our own in the way we have come to claim them as our own. As a point of emphasis, the deception is that society is us; we're not in it. I feel bravado in my cotton tee because cotton t-shirts are regarded by society as bravado. I will therefore justify the importance of cotton tees because they bring to me other people's recognition and familiar ways of acting toward me as bravado.

The world is predictable; I know how people will think, feel, and behave in relation to me on the basis of my cotton tee. I don't need to defend something that's not really me. When I'm not identified with my cotton t-shirt, then I can wear it or not wear it, whatever I choose. I can create a new standard that won't make me miserable if I don't have a cotton tee and will enable me to tolerate people that don't wear t-shirts.

The idea here is that we are limited in the ways we know and value who we are (for the sake of knowing what to do in relation to things and people). At an extremely reflexive level, think about how we never question our familiarity and identifications with our basic organismic features—we have two eyes, we're bipedal, and so on. It all feels just like us. When we are able to stand back and feel the strangeness of who we are, then we have found society.

Prince: "Everything You Do Is Success"

In Prince's song "Cream," he declares that everything he does is success. This is the social self, the ego, the sense of pride that shouts, "Look at me! I did it! I made it! I'm a success!" But beware: This pride is society making us feel that we are okay because we've provided it with what it values. And if we lose what it values, we lose ourselves. Once we are aware of the social self, once we can recognize it, we are able to see it for what it is: simply society's way of ensuring our survival.

But the social self is not who we really are; it's an expression of what we are. It's like the little kid who is enthralled with himself and his ability to swim. He's so proud—gloating, taking credit for doing fantastic feats—that he forgets that his life jacket is actually supporting him. The real self is the foundation for everything that we are and do, and when we return to that alternative and fundamental self-awareness, we are what we really are. This self is invulnerable to losing itself because it recognizes that it never possessed a self in the first place. The self is the thing that can possess.

Sociotherapy: Breaking Down Defenses

So, what's the point? The point is that sociology shows us that our self-regard is really social regard, and our self-esteem is a barometer for telling us how well we are cooperating by society's standards. We are constantly up and down, each day, measuring how well we are being society.

This cannot be the final word or the end of the story about who we are, but it is what we are when we are not aware of sociology's essential insights. Society does not have the last say about who we are. We are not reduced to little individual versions of society. Sociology is like a sociotherapy because it leads us to the realization of what it is to be individual. Sociology leads us to say, This can't be all there is to it, to me, to what I am!

Later in this book (Chapters 8, 9, and 10), we will discuss how sociology's second insight is to return us to a sensitivity of ourselves that frees us from depending on society for our sense of *I* in the world. Sociology teaches us that we must judge in order to know what to do with ourselves in relation to others; we come to rank and sort people in our judgments. We also come to rank and sort ourselves. Thinness is Theresa, until she sees stratification as social structure. In seeing social structure, sociology has taught us the discipline of experiencing ourselves as the things judging, not as the judgments.

GLOSSARY

ascribed Describes socially valued characteristics or attributes unrelated to merit or achievement; assigned qualities, such as gender and race.

attribute A characteristic of someone or something that society says to value.

conflict theory of stratification An explanation of how the principle of stratification operates that stresses competition over valued resources as the basis for human relations; the allocation of socially valued resources according to who has power in the social system.

functional theory of stratification An explanation of how the principle of stratification operates according to which society's rules for the allocation of wealth, power, and prestige are founded on achievement and matching important roles with scarce talents.

inequality The condition when entire categories of the population have different life chances to obtain social rewards (wealth, power, prestige).

power The possession of influence over others because of having attributes society values. For example, parents have influence over their children; this is usually a fair allocation of power because parents can use their knowledge and experience to guide their children. But when fewer women than men hold executive positions, regardless of individual qualifications, this is an unfair allocation of power, one based on ascription rather than merit.

prestige Respect or esteem granted on the basis of attributes society values.

social mobility Movement from one social status to another; the ability to change one's status and thus one's value in society.

socially desirable resources Those attributes valued by society that result in wealth, power, and prestige.

sociotherapy Learning through sociology to experience a sense of identity, or self, apart from one's social value; seeing that social structure creates the ego, or personality; a sense of self based on giving up what society designates as valuable; seeing that one has a social value but is not reduced to that social value.

stratification, principle of The principle that regulates who should have what of the desirable things in life (wealth, power, and prestige) and under what conditions; rules that establish what to value and how much. These rules are known to us in personality, as demonstrated by how we judge others (good or bad, right or wrong, smart or dumb, etc.) and also how we judge ourselves by these value standards. For example, a man may feel unattractive because he has thinning hair and a woman because she is not rail thin.

wealth Monetary reward received because one has attributes valued by the group; denotes economic status.

NOTES

1. Reprinted with permission of the author.
2. Reprinted with permission of the author.
3. This section is based on Lynn M. Mulkey, *Sociology of Education: Theoretical and Empirical Investigations* (Orlando, FL: Harcourt Brace Jovanovich, 1993), pp. 127–128. Theories explain the nature of principles, particularly as to their stratification characteristics. Therefore, the principle of stratification operates in conjunction with all other principles of sociology and is evidenced in discussion of the theoretical interpretations of the natures of other principles.
4. This section is based on Mulkey, pp. 128–129.
5. For extended commentaries on this question, see Kingsley Davis and Wilbert E. Moore, "Some Principles of Stratification," *American Sociological Review*, 10 (April 1945): 242–249; Kingsley Davis, *Human Society* (New York: Macmillan, 1949), 366–368; Dennis H. Wrong, "The Functional Theory of Stratification: Some Neglected Considerations," *American Sociological Review*, 24 (December 1959): 772–782; and Melvin M. Tumin, "Some Principles of Stratification: A Critical Analysis," *American Sociological Review*, 18 (August 1953): 387–393.
6. Max Weber, *Max Weber: Essays in Sociology*, edited by H. H. Gerth and C. Wright Mills (New York: Oxford University Press, 1946).

6

DEVIATING FROM WHAT WE'RE TAUGHT TO WANT, GET, AND BE
Seeing Social Control as Social Structure

◆ WHO DECIDES WHAT'S NORMAL?

Pink Floyd and "Breaking with the Pack"

Nathaniel Hawthorne's Hester Prynne and *The Scarlet Letter*

◆ "SOCIETY MADE ME DO IT"

Tossed in the Clink for Drug Possession, Resisting Arrest, and Nosepicking

The Beverly Hills Homeless at Home for the Holidays

*M*eet Pearl. She is not who you think she is, and, more importantly, she is not who she thinks she is. She is not an individual as much as she is society. As with other people we've met in this book, the transformation in our understanding of who Pearl is—to herself and to others—is what sociology is about. It is a new perception.

Society takes Pearl as amorphous protoplasm and directs her to feel and behave in specific ways. Society has to tell her what to do with her organismic drives; it places them under the supervision or control of social rules. Pearl's sex drive, for instance, can be expressed (as romantic love, as pure recreation, or as an emotionally detached act of prostitution), suppressed, sublimated, and repressed. Of course, considering the sexual alternatives is intellectual for Pearl. All she knows and feels is that she doesn't want to have sex until she is married—and the person must be a "him."

My virginity was not an issue until I came to college. I did it for Mom. Since I was young, I can remember my mother pounding into my head that sex is something you do only when you are married—

there is no other option. She would say, "No, you just do not do that. It's not nice. Sex is something you save for your husband. Nobody wants used goods." Mom pointed out that I would be labeled a "slut" if I had sex before marriage or possibly could become pregnant and ruin my life. Even worse, I could get a disease of some sort or be used simply for my reputation.

All of these terrifying ramifications that could stem from one act of premarital intercourse were repeatedly stated to me, so much so that I simply accepted that virginity is the only way to be. My acceptance of this rule focused my attention on incidents that reinforced what I had been taught. I witnessed friends in high school act promiscuously and then get reputations, used for sex, and then dumped or even pregnant and in need of an abortion. One of my exboyfriends even got the girl he dated right after me pregnant, and he dropped out of school to get married. My high school friends would say things like, "Oh, Pearl, you are better off the way you are. It's not worth it."

My dilemma to have or not to have sex became an issue my freshman year in my first serious relationship. It was not acceptable for a relationship so intense and happy to lack sex. I am worried about my ability to let go of the guilt I have come to associate with sexual activity. My learned way to react to sexual feelings is not to engage in intercourse with a man before marriage.[1]

To understand why Pearl feels so strongly about having sex only in marriage, we must know something about society. Fundamentally, society embodies itself as Pearl's personality—the consolidation of the group's instructions about how she should feel and act toward things and people in the world. Those instructions about what to do with her sexuality are called "mate" instructions. Society might use sex to achieve family behavior, establishing courtship and mating instructions that bring certain people together to ensure propagation and caretaking of children. Pearl perceives her feelings and actions as inherent, natural, belonging to her. But she first belongs to society. So we understand her when we understand society.

We ask again, If Pearl is society, then what is individual about her? Once we see society as Pearl, we unsee society; we move to another level of vision, or self-perception, that allows us to realize what it means to be an individual. In perceiving ourselves as antecedent to and separate from our social value, we can evaluate and act on our learned social behaviors according to a new standard.

*W*hen Pearl proclaims she "did it for Mom," Mom is really society and is now Pearl. The internalized rule is now Pearl's preference, a feature of her personality. We have to ask, then, what could it possibly mean to be an individual, to have some choice in the matter of one's sexual drive?

By coming up with novel ways (society's directions) to defer sexual gratification, the human animal has an enhanced ability to adapt to its surroundings; it does not have to respond immediately, in only one way, or at all. Ultimately, the human has the capacity to override her biology; that is, her sense of well-being no longer depends directly or even indirectly on the fulfillment of material or social needs.

The human who has realized that capacity is an *individual* because nothing, absolutely nothing, in her perception determines her sense of who she is. This is the individual who can be in the world as a giving, not getting, person. Society would be a loving and perfect community if each person would not worry about her needs. It isn't that the person is not aware of her physical needs for survival, such as food and water; she just doesn't worry about them because she defines herself beyond the material sense. And, in not worrying about these needs, the individual does what she has to gracefully, without effort, in the best interests of all. In seeing and unseeing social structure, Pearl can conform or not conform but under a new auspices. It doesn't matter that she "prefers" sexual activity only on rainy days if she is happy whether she has it or not.

The social fact is, though, that even the most personal feelings and sensations are not really under our direction. In terms of sexual feelings, society tells us to pay attention to them and whom to be attracted to and when. Society takes that amorphous protoplasm and styles it. That styling is evident when I feel disgust at seeing someone masturbate in public or at thinking of parents copulating with their offspring. Imagine, though, not that this disgust is the way it is, but that, without society's instructions and dictates, the boundaries on our behavior would be quite different. For the human, even when it comes to human sexuality, she would be at a loss with what to do with herself. An unsocialized human being might not recognize or give attention to her sexual feelings; the unsocialized person is undifferentiated. The disgust is society's because it needs to regulate sexuality toward its own interests. Homosexual behavior, for example, may bring a judgment of another's worth—but this is social value. We may respect a murderer as a human being but also understand that our judgment of that person at the social level is disapproval for a behavior that threatens the relations that protect our survival.

WHO DECIDES WHAT'S NORMAL?

We will attempt to understand Pearl's behavior as a response to yet another principle of sociology: *social control and deviance*. Pearl has the appearance of conformity; the question is, Why isn't she more idiosyncratic in her behavior?

Society exacts conformity after it decides which behaviors are normal and which are deviant, although note here that we are not individual simply by deviating from the rules; we are just conforming to deviant rules. We need the group to direct our behavior whether those directions lead us to deviance or conformity.

We rarely ask why certain behaviors are punished and others are rewarded. Once the rules become us, we feel anxious and guilty if we do not conform; we feel uncomfortable with ourselves. Deviance—behavior that is bothersome to most people—is not inherent; it is a relative phenomenon. So we might also ask whether deviance is defined through a general consensus of values or whether a conflict of values exists between those who have the power to apply definitions of deviance and those who do not.

We will examine the orderliness and predictable nature of our human world by looking at some more of the rules that make it so— how societies decide what counts as deviance and what actions are taken to get people to conform to social conventions. We will investigate how the principle of social control and deviance operates by looking at how various theories explain its operation, such as control theory, cultural transmission theory, and structural strain theory.[2] These theories account for many issues, including the regulation of sexual behavior. What counts as deviance in this context? What fosters conformity? The principle of social control and deviance, as it concerns several major youth issues, is applied in discussing these theories; reciprocally, these issues reveal something of the nature of the principle of social control and deviance.

Besides solving the problem of who gets what through stratification rules, every human group must solve another problem: It must define for its members what is acceptable and unacceptable in their relatedness with each other.[3] *Social control and deviance* refers to that aspect of rule making that orients the feelings and actions of a person in terms of rightness and wrongness. Social control and deviance singles out features of our experience, names them, and places a judgment on them. As with Pearl, coitus with whom and when are decided by the group: "This is good; this isn't." Sex with your father is something we give a name to, *incest,* and sex against your will is something we name *rape.*

These are unacceptable behaviors. "Note them, feel this way about them," says society.

The value of an item as acceptable or nonacceptable is not dichotomous or clearcut, one or the other. It is on a continuum, and society delineates and conveys these shades of conformity and deviance. You're not perverted in your sexual behavior if you learn to be attracted to people more or less your age, but an attraction between a 40-year-old and a 9-year-old reflects the internalization of a rule defining deviant sexual behavior: pedophilia. In this way, society coordinates our behavior.

Deviance is when persons act out a rule that constitutes a violation of important expectations for behavior. *Social control* refers to making behavioral proscriptions as well as prescriptions, including rules that deem good the punishment of unacceptable behavior. We learn to manage ourselves as normal or as deviant, but we need rules for both. At a very subjective level, the principle of social control and deviance can be detected as a person's sense of guilt or fear of external ridicule or punishment. At the societal level, the principle operates as collective expectations, codified and objectified as social structure, so that individuals, according to their nominal status or position in the group, know which behaviors meet with the group's approval and which do not. Sometimes people do not internalize the rules isomorphically; this means that we don't reflect the rules as if they have been branded on our cognition and emotion. We even have rules for feeling and acting that guarantee the management of people who do not learn the meanings of conformity and deviance. For example, a serial killer may have failed to internalize that taking the life of a human is unacceptable; society will define attitudes and behaviors toward this person that lead to her conformity to the group.

Pink Floyd and "Breaking with the Pack"

Now, what about Pearl's virginity? Pink Floyd, a rock group that began in the 1960s, is still heard singing a song about "breaking with the pack." Why doesn't Pearl break with the pack—society's expectations— especially in the name of sex?

Sociologists are accustomed (through their learned conformity) to ask the question of when and why some persons employ their learned rules for deviance as opposed to those for conformity. Sociologists give less notice to how quickly or how deeply felt and attached we are to what feels so much our own—whether in our reaction to people who exhibit deviant behavior or to ourselves when we think of deviating. Again, the group has implemented its plan of action as us. Pearl feels naturally and justifiably sure of what to do with her sexuality.

Societal regulation of human sexual behavior includes the analysis of how such regulation manages a person's sexuality during her life course.[4] Chronologically, *adolescence* is an attribute of persons designated by society to include specific directions for feeling and acting sexual. The principle of social control and deviance operates, theoretically, in several ways, to account for adolescent sexuality.

Control theory asserts that the human has an unbridled sexual energy that must be harnessed by social regulations or else society will become saddled with rampant undesirable sexual activity. Adolescent sexual behavior, according to this perspective, is correlated with values and norms transmitted via the family, religious, peer, and community organization. Sociologists have investigated how, given hormonal levels of adolescents, rules of social control regulate these biological factors differently for boys than for girls. Society tells us, more or less, what to do with our hormones.

Another perspective, *cultural transmission* theory, articulates how society orders human sexuality variously according to the subgroup context that its members comprise—by race, ethnicity, and class. What feels to Pearl like the only and right thing to do emanates from society's broader plan of human relatedness, including whose interests are served and how.

A *structural strain* analysis of society's management of human sexuality not only stresses how but also why a subgroup has the expectations it does. For example, in subcultures of poverty, where persons socially cannot define their contribution to the group economically, motherhood becomes an alternative definition of the social self. Early coitus and out-of-wedlock parenthood are normative for persons in the subgroup but deviant for persons in the mainstream group.

Labeling theorists explain that persons come to behave according to the role deviant. When a person commits a primary act of what society calls inappropriate behavior and identifies the person as "deviant," that individual accepts the label and behaves according to deviant expectations. Frequently, children who are placed in special education classes, whether for giftedness or limitations, are recognized and come to recognize themselves according to the judgments society assigns to what it socially pays attention to as cognitive performance. Note that as society, we are not individualistic by deviating from it but rather we learn rules for deviance or conformity.

Functional theorists attempt to explain when and why the expression of human sexuality is dysfunctional to the system as a whole, and *conflict* theorists explain how the many versions of sexual attractions and activities promote the interests of some and not others. Terms such as *prostitution* and *date rape* name forms of sexual relatedness where some people benefit at the expense of others.

Pearl's virginity can be accounted for by control theory because her conscience is strong in declaring society's judgment of teen sex. Cultural transmission theory does less in explaining Pearl's behavior because she exhibits staunch conformity to the mainstream culture. Structural strain theory explains Pearl's behavior as conformist; she has adequate resources to achieve mainstream goals and doesn't need to deviate from conventionally defined goals and means.

With all these theories, we are inclined to think of ourselves as mere puppets of society and particularly its instructions about what is deviant and what is normal. But if being a virgin is being Pearl, then when and if she breaks society's rules about sexuality, she will really break Pearl. If she violates society, she will actually violate herself. That is the guilt Pearl referred to in her opening excerpt. She doesn't know or feel secure about trying another way of getting around in the group; she feels like a person when she directs or experiences her sexuality in the form or manner society designates.

Nathaniel Hawthorne's Hester Prynne and *The Scarlet Letter*

Pearl has two choices: She can develop an identity based on the negative or positive regard of society, or she can realize that society does not tell her who she really is. Hester Prynne, the central character in Nathaniel Hawthorne's *The Scarlet Letter*,[5] finds through committing adultery not the condemnation and annihilation of herself but the transcendence of society and her self as she knew it as society. She comes to evaluate the act of adultery on new terms by disidentifying with being the adulteress. By unseeing society, she can either commit suicide and admit total rejection or she can use the event to come to a new self-perception. Thus, Hester might conform or not conform to society according to a new standard. No longer would she be driven to adultery because she would see that having or not having sex with the person she loves is not required for her being and fulfillment.

"SOCIETY MADE ME DO IT"

Logically, we arrive at another query: Is the *I* that deviates *us* or *society?* Every time I walk past a homeless person in New York City's Penn

Station, I ask myself, Who is to blame for this poverty and alienation: the individual or society?

Tossed in the Clink for Drug Possession, Resisting Arrest, and Nosepicking

Deviance—drug possession, resisting arrest, and nosepicking—can have two outcomes. The first outcome, to be determined by the odds, is to accept society's definition of us and its resources in bringing compliance to it. The second outcome is to see that the very lack of resources brings us to question whether society has the final word about who we are. When asked about who they want to be, poor high school students in Brooklyn might say, "A celebrity." But few realize the essential insights of sociology: You have to give up the social self to achieve what it is to be a real self, or individual. When you don't have to be a celebrity to be a person, then you are more likely to be a celebrity.

The Beverly Hills Homeless at Home for the Holidays

So, whose fault is it that the homeless house themselves in Penn Station: the individual's or society's? Both deviance and conformity reflect society and its rules. The various theories on deviance say that people break the rules because, in one way or another, they are reacting to the demands society places on them to be selves, or persons.

For example, consider Pearl's virginity. Her conformity or her deviance can now be interpreted by sociology's essential insights. Society stakes the first claim on who she is, but it also makes available, developmentally, a way for her to stake the final claim on who she is. Initially, we see social structure—that Pearl is not who she thinks she is. Her claim to virginity is really society's claim to virginity. We see how social structure operates to define the person according to its procedures for alignment with the group. In seeing that social structure is Pearl, she is brought to another level of self-understanding. If she is society, she must ask, then, what about her is individual?

In seeing who she is as social structure, Pearl can grasp the opportunity to unsee (the expression of self rather than equating herself with her social value). Nothing, including sexuality, *is* us. Sexuality is the opportunity for expressing something greater, and, in finding this grounding of being, provisions for expressing our sexuality are evaluated on a new basis, where we are free to conform or deviate because we need neither.

Now, think as a sociologist. Meet Lori. What would you say to her?

Eighteen years ago on Labor Day weekend, something happened that changed my life. I was four years old at the time, listening to records in my brother's room. After I was done, I left the room. My brother told me that I had to shut off the record player. There was no "on" and "off" switch, so the only way that it turned on and off was by plugging it in and out. I tried to pull the plug, but I wasn't strong enough. I even remembered trying to pull it out with my feet. I still couldn't do it. My brother yelled at me, saying that if I could plug it in, I could unplug it.

Trying not to get into trouble, I decided I could pull it out with my teeth. As I bit the plug, I got electrocuted. My brother saw me with the plug in my mouth and screamed for my parents. I believe his scream made me drop the plug. My whole bottom lip turned silver. My parents rushed me to the doctor, and he said I was lucky to be alive.

I grew up with a big scar on the bottom side of my lip. According to society, that was not normal. The children in my elementary school would make fun of me because, when I smiled, the right side of my lip didn't go up like the left side. So I stopped smiling. I thought that, if I didn't smile, you couldn't see it as much. I had plastic surgery three times since age twelve to improve my scar, but the nerves were burnt and there was no way of fixing them. When I smile, that side of my lip still does not go up, and I have a big complex because of it. I feel that I'm socially deviant. I smile minimally, and society says I should smile.[6]

Notice that Lori is judging herself by society's standard, as it is now her own, her personality; the only value she finds in herself is society's. What, potentially, is the end of this story of Lori and who she is?

GLOSSARY

attachment to deviance or conformity roles Awareness of oneself as individual simply by viewing oneself as deviant rather than seeing both deviance and conformity as sociostructural forms, or roles, and being attached to either or both.

deviance Behavior that society arbitrarily defines as inappropriate or undesirable.

normal Behavior that society arbitrarily defines as acceptable or desirable.

social control and deviance, principle of The principle for interaction that specifies how much or to what degree some human or environmental attribute is acceptable or unacceptable.

social control and deviance, theories of Explanations of the operation of the principle of social control and deviance (why people conform and deviate), including control theory, structural strain theory, labeling theory, and differential association theory.

NOTES

1. Reprinted with permission of the author.   ·
2. For additional information on cultural transmission, structural strain, control, and labeling theories, respectively, see Edwin Sutherland, *Principles of Criminology* (Philadelphia: Lippincott, 1939); Robert K. Merton, *Social Theory and Social Structure* (New York: Free Press, 1968), p. 194; Travis Hirschi, *Causes of Delinquency* (Berkeley: University of California Press, 1969); Edwin M. Lemert, *Social Psychology* (New York: McGraw-Hill, 1951) and *Human Deviance, Social Problems, and Social Control* (Englewood Cliffs, NJ: Prentice Hall, 1967); and Howard Becker, *Outsider: Studies in the Sociology of Deviance* (New York: Free Press, 1963).
3. This section is based on Lynn M. Mulkey, *Sociology of Education: Theoretical and Empirical Investigations* (Orlando, FL: Harcourt Brace Jovanovich, 1993), pp. 199–200.
4. This section is based on Mulkey, pp. 204–205.
5. Nathaniel Hawthorne, *The Scarlet Letter* (New York: Penguin Books, 1983; originally published in 1850).
6. Reprinted with permission of the author.

7

CHANGING WHAT WE WANT, WHAT WE GET, AND WHO WE ARE
Seeing Social Change as Social Structure

♦ SOME THINGS CHANGE, AND SOME THINGS STAY THE SAME

From Racist to Liberal

From Turkey to Türkiye, from Mendelssohn to Wagner

♦ AFFIRMATION VERSUS CONFIRMATION

What You Can't See *Will* Hurt You:
Censorship in the Clintonian Nineties

*M*eet Bill. He finds that his addiction is not to a drug but to society.

When I first began weight lifting, the presence of anabolic steroids was scarce but steadily became more available. By the time I was 18, I had already done a cycle (several-week period of steroid use) and saw exceptional results. I started with relatively safe oral drugs, but within one year, I began "stacking" (taking more than one drug at a time) these steroids in alarming dosages. I felt increasingly aggressive and oftentimes depressed. Well aware of the dangers of steroid use, I began to accept my behavior as normal because I coveted the so-called benefits that accompanied the use of the drugs.

Eventually, I dropped out of school and spent thousands of dollars obtaining steroids. Outside of the physical gains I had made and the approval of them were the tremendous losses: money, friends, and time I could have been spending in school, working toward other goals. When I ceased usage, I experienced withdrawal symptoms such as decreased sex drive, fatigue, depression, and a desire to initiate steroid use again. Only by removing myself from the weight-lifting crowd I chose to associate with was I able to overcome these symptoms and get my life in gear.

Drug free for four years, I am now working in a health club. Being in this environment again has brought me to realize the dependence I had on steroids and, now I see, really on society; I have witnessed scores of people fall into the same trap I did. Many give in, as I did, to peer pressure that exists when a friend or training partner begins to use steroids to achieve society's standards for physical attractiveness. Unfortunately, most medical problems from this dependence will surface later in life, and the naiveté of youth as well as the instant gratification mentality of the users can be devastating.[1]

Meet Jeff. He says, now that he has "taken sociology with Mulkey," he knows that society is him. It follows that, if he had a different family atmosphere, he would be a different person. What is provocative about Jeff's story is that he attributes alcoholism (another addiction) and its effects to his family, not to the individual (his father) but to the individual as society.

Growing up in rural, upstate New York, my life seemed quite simple. My family consisted of Mom, Dad, my sister, and me. To a stranger looking in on us from the outside, our family situation may seem ideal. This, however, was not the case.

My parents were married at a young age, and I was born before either one of them was 20 years old. After my arrival, my mother took on the role of housewife while my father became the breadwinner. At the age of 5, my family and I moved to a quiet town in the country. My father moved from job to job, trying to make a living good enough to support everyone. He began to drink heavily when I was about 7 years old. At first, it was only beer, but over the years, it gradually progressed to harder alcohol when beer was no longer enough.

I never realized that there was a problem until I was about 15. I used to find empty liquor bottles hidden around the house. My mother didn't like when my father would drink. She never would say anything directly to him, not until the problem was too serious. The drinking problem is the main reason for their two separations and finally their divorce, which began the day I left for college.

I always questioned whether or not I would be a different person if alcoholism had not been present in my home. Alcohol was used by my father to escape from the troubles of everyday life. . . . I was socialized with this in mind. . . . This helps me to understand myself.[2]

Another one of my students whose brother, at the age of 33, committed suicide, remarked that his brother let society have the final word about who he was. He left a blue album behind, a diary, for people to read about how no one recognized the value of his social self, how important he really was according to the accomplishments he had listed.

In the following discussion, we will consider how we make society a better place: How do we structure our relations to eliminate societal and individual problems? The issue is less that society has to change its standards for what it values and more that we must change our relationship to those standards.

*S*ociology's task is to reveal how society has the power and responsibility to initially but not finally determine what we want, what we get, and who we are. Our society sets its standards, and they become us. So how do we change what society teaches us to prefer? Certainly, a two-year-old has no choice in taking on the reality of society. He is simply given to understand that you call this human "Mom," this one "Dad," and this is how you should feel about them, what you should expect from them, and how you should act toward them.

At best, when we come to see social structure as us, we understand that our choices are society's choices as us. And then, what comes to view in our self-perception is our self observing the conforming and socially styled social self. We don't change by trying to change our learned preferences. Their hold on us is automatically loosened when we are able to conform or not conform by experiencing these proclivities as expressions *for what* we are, not *what* we are. I understand my love of matzo ball soup, but I'm able to feel content as a person with or without it.

SOME THINGS CHANGE, AND SOME THINGS STAY THE SAME

Sociology's first essential insight is how much we are the group, and when we see that (and this is sociology's second insight), we can we realize what it is to be an individual.

It seems that the principle of social change never changes.[3] Theoretically, it operates in a variety of ways, but fundamentally, it operates at two levels. The crucial theory, for our purposes, posits that social change facilitates and reflects the orientation and degree of self-interest of the society's members. Different realizations of what it is to be individual have different implications for social change.

As is true of the other principles of sociology, the operation of the principle of social change is lawlike in its function, but its description is less precise and determinate and its operation requires a variety of explanations. Sociologists theorize that social change results from the interaction of a number of factors, including the physical environment (the rules for living in the arctic regions vary from the rules for living on a tropical island); cultural innovation (discovery, invention, and diffusion); population; technology; and social movements (collective social action by large numbers of people).[4]

One theoretical account of why humans change the forms of their relatedness is founded on *social movement*. Dissatisfaction with current arrangements brings about four types of rearrangements:

1. A *regressive* movement attempts to restore human structures of cooperation to historically previous ones. In American education, disillusionment with the current formal organization to meet the educational needs of a racially and ethnically diverse population has led to a back-to-basics movement.
2. A *reform* movement attempts to change specific aspects of social structure while leaving the residual and main portion intact. Again, using an illustration from education, compensatory education programs are implemented to provide auxiliary avenues to meet the needs of subgroups of the population not served by the general arrangements. Currently, an effort exists to "detrack" students in schools; homogeneous ability grouping does not seem to serve the needs of some students.
3. A *revolutionary* movement is the pervasive reordering of social structure.
4. A *utopian* social movement seeks to establish the social conditions of an ideal society.

These theoretical formulations of how the principle of social change operates do not explain how and why these movements begin. Under what circumstances do persons become dissatisfied with the existing social order? Usually, this happens through degrees of self-interest or disinterest.

Some other explanations of the operation of the principle of social change are the functional, conflict, sociocultural-evolution, and levels of change theories. For the *functional* theorist, the ways in which whole societies change instructions for our relatedness is according to the maintenance of equilibrium of the social system. Society becomes a changed set of rules, depending on its increasing differentiation and complexity. When, for example, the societal illiteracy rate rises because the educational system is failing, strain is put on the whole system, and this stimulates an adjustment in the rules to return the system to stability.

A *conflict* theorist claims that social movement depends on the tension between competing interest groups over valued and scarce resources. Social rules reflect the interests of the dominant group and change would occur as the attempt to eliminate privilege and elitism. A *sociocultural-evolutionist* explains the principle of social change as the tendency for a society to become increasingly complex over time; social structure ordering our relationships would change to accommodate an agricultural versus an industrial or postindustrial system of subsistence, for instance.

Perhaps to better understand the principle of social change, we may need a synthesis of explanations. No one theory presented so far seems to adequately account for social change nor can all the theories together tell us with precision where and how social change begins. I offer a theory of *level of social change* that posits that massive social systems (the consolidation of instructions on how to feel and act) cannot change unless someone designs the change. Actually, this theory suggests that only one person can initiate change. But how?

Several social thinkers have linked social change to the individual by way of *consciousness.* Scholars such as Karl Marx, Max Weber, Pitirim Sorokin, Auguste Comte, and Talcott Parsons[5] explain that the rules of society change over time based on the type of reality of which its members are conscious. Marx, for example, says that one's relationship to others changes in relation to changes in economic or material condition. Weber explains that beliefs are antecedent to material conditions and determine change in the human's association with people and things. Sorokin says that values on sense experience (science), spiritual and religious awareness, or the combination of sensate and ideational consciousness are the broad determinants of individual human action. Comte states that the evolution of society is the evolution of the human mind from theological (fictitious) to metaphysical (abstract) to scientific (positive); each stage of development is reflected in social organization.

What remains unclear in each explication is under what conditions society determines individual consciousness or consciousness determines society. Can one individual be separate of his known ways of relating (society) long enough to change the rules of behavior on which he depends? I speculate yes. One person can change society by way of change in his awareness of society as a determinant of his behavior. The human can, at any point, eject himself from society—that is, he can realize his identification with it and, in doing that, can change society. Society reflects social self-defense until the disinterested self changes it.

Two kinds of social change seem possible for an individual: change in the provision of social structure and change in one's attachment to the provisions. Bill and Jeff, for example, might find alternative ways to define themselves, but they may still depend on the new roles in the same ways they depended on the old roles. Alternatively, they might realize that any patterns of preferences or habits can change in a moment through the realization that nothing out there—drugs and alcohol included—is necessary for creating and maintaining who they are at another level of self-understanding.

Change in the principles of being, of selfhood, is understandable when we see it as the application of two distinctive sets of principles. Each set of principles brings a specific type of social activity. The first set operates *in* society and the second set operates at another level and is reflected in society—*in* it but not *of* it.

From Racist to Liberal

To illustrate the two types of changes in the rules, we might think about someone changing from a racist to a liberal—but this assumes that he is one or the other. People want to kill when they are criticized and are hesitant to accept compliments because they feel they are the standard. But how can you be subject to destruction—or construction, for that matter—by big ocean waves when you live in the air? The principles that govern our social being are separate from those that govern *being*. We are not our social roles, and in knowing that, we choose an appropriate expression without depending on either.

For example, *work* is something people *do*. It is serving by law: Under certain conditions, this is what you get (the principle of stratification). The shift in one's perception—from being society to the being that makes being in society possible at all—transforms work into another occasion of service. The notion of "my money for my work" becomes the exhilaration of being able to give or serve, and the money is inevitable.

This is what I call a *horizontal* adaptation rather than a *vertical* adaptation. Horizontal adaptation occurs when the social self is able to achieve a certain integration of the many social forms. Vertical adaptation occurs when the social self experiences itself as an *I* (the subject) minus the *me* (the self as object), or the direct experience of itself. Each self-construction has specific consequences with implications for two types of clinical therapies, or mechanisms for change: One *resocializes* the individual; the other *desocializes* the individual.

From Turkey to Türkiye, from Mendelssohn to Wagner

The *I as me* construction of self has a distinctive set of consequences for persons and for society. Personal problems can be traced to self-objectification, or to how we identify ourselves as objects defined by society rather than with the self that made this objectification possible in the first place. Seeing social structure is seeing the process of self-objectification. We have talked about the process of seeing in more detail in other chapters, but for now, know that psychological and societal problems among human beings are really problems of self-objectification.

To the extent that the group and the self are experienced as one, the judgment of one's group comes to constitute self-esteem, an evaluation of one's self. The social self elicits from the individual an awareness of himself as constituted by his child, his spouse, his home. The self becomes his family, his gender, his race. This feeling of self as these things produce prejudice, racism, sexism, and war as defenses of what it thinks are itself.

The problem is one of self-alienation because of the social identification with the self. The sense of self depends on defeating, taking, and having and—when threatened by nothing to defeat, take, and have—is depressed, suicidal, or desperate as opposed to content with just exactly what it is. The implications of these consequences for change are therapeutic interventions for adaptation through horizontal change: resocialization. This means that if you can't be a self by living up to one definition society offers, you can shift to another. Note, however, that you will still be in society, changing from one thing to another but at the same level of attachment to or identification with society—from Turkey to Türkiye and from Mendelssohn to Wagner. Turkey did not want to define itself as "American," so it changed the spelling of its name to *Türkiye*. Israel will not permit the playing of Wagner's music because it represents support of someone German. In the past, Germany would not permit the playing of Mendelssohn's music because he was Jewish. These are clearly changes but at the same level of identification with or determination by society.

Losing ourselves is an inevitable outcome of self-objectification; to do so means the individual is one who is separate from his direct experience of himself, and he identifies with, attaches to, equates himself with, and becomes one with the objectified self. Self-alienation estranges and fragments persons for the sake of cooperation. Our sense of self always depends on the group. Take the example presented earlier: If a woman defines herself by her ability to have a child, she will lose herself if she doesn't have a child; she will not know how to act and feel in the world. She will also defend social activities that guarantee that women are women by having children.

When a person cannot live up to himself—internalized standards for being a self—he cannot access the normal repertoires for feeling like a self. The consequences of losing one's social self are so-called social problems such as alcoholism and drug abuse. Alcohol makes an individual forget a socially incompetent self and induces the experience of a competent social self. This way of understanding oneself is transmitted through socialization intergenerationally. One student expressed this in stating, "Although my father died when I was 10 years old, I definitely feel that I was not too young to be affected by his alcoholism." A student demonstrating poor cognitive performance might enhance his ego by attributing his incompetence to lack of effort and will avoid admitting he is not able. Society values cognitive facility; we are not valued for just being—we are valued for being what society expects.

◆ AFFIRMATION VERSUS CONFIRMATION

Two ways of experiencing ourselves are possible. One way is through *self-affirmation;* the other way is through *self-confirmation.* The self-affirmed person is always anxious and dependent on society to let him know when he is acceptable. The self-confirmed person, by grounding his identity within himself, is free to gracefully perform his social functions. The self is confirmed while the social self is affirmed.

The implication of these consequences for the individual and for society calls for clinical therapies that are resocialization or horizontal adaptations—taking on alternative ways to feel and act, as in the case of recovering from divorce or the loss of a loved one. Divorce represents not so much a breakdown in the rules of the group but in personality. Through marriage, persons become habituated to sharing themselves in particular ways and degrees with others; when they can no longer rely on this continuity of their experience, they seek divorce. But as a result, they become out of control about who they are and what they should do in relation to people and things in the world.

Therapeutic intervention for this consequence of loss of social self simply gets the individual to find alternative social roles. But it does not free him from his dependence on the group for security; in this sense, divorce leaves the human determined by the group. The person, alternatively and developmentally, however, has the possibility for a second type of self-construction: from the *I as me* (equated with society) to the *I as I* (expressing through society). If we don't see the alternative, we can never experience it. Seeing, first, and then unseeing means that what you can't see *will* hurt you; you will be in the world anxiously defending the way to be a self.

What You Can't See *Will* Hurt You: Censorship in the Clintonian Nineties

Moving in forward gear and reverse gear at the same time is impossible. Likewise, if we are in the "getting" mode, we cannot imagine giving. We see ourselves in society—for example, in American society in the Clintonian nineties—in terms of what society can do for us. Society's feelings and actions regarding censorship—whether it pertains to pollution, aggression and war, crime, sexual preference, physical and mental health, gender and age inequality—become our censorship. We keep trying to change the world so that it's better for us. We want to be celebrities, to be recognized, to borrow our worth and being from others, yet few persons think of giving up themselves for their fulfillment. We can't see that giving solves the problem of getting, and what we can't see will hurt us.

Sociology makes available another vision, that of the hero. The hero has a different mindset—he does not value people or things in terms of what they can do for him. The hero finds respite within because he realizes his thoughts and feelings are not his to begin with. The hero doesn't give up himself but rather the false perception of himself—the perception that brings one kind of consequences to his own and society's well-being. The hero can enjoy all things, regardless of their instrumental value, but not be attached to them. A blade of grass is no less sacred than a diamond in a bank vault.

To change society is to change in oneself the perception of society. For example, we make the cockroach less valuable than the Masaratti until we realize that things are what they are before we value them instrumentally. We *lose* something when we think we *had* it in the first place.

The social self-construction of self has different consequences for persons and society than the self-construction of self. This second capacity for self-construction releases the human from identification with the world and replaces it with an identification with the ground of being. In this mode of self-awareness, the human exhibits the optimum degree of adaptation because he can sustain a sense of himself despite any external, material, or social threat and can change society because he doesn't feel dependent on it. The implications of this kind of self-construction are for fostering the continual practice, the discipline, an eternal vigilance of vertical change—change not in the part one plays in society but change in one's relationship to society. This vertical change is *desocialization* in contrast to *resocialization,* the conscious act of the *I* in saying to every social situation, "I am but not this."

Sociology's insights—unseeing social structure—requires, in every way, seeing social structure. The new sensitivity to what it means to be a self is an awareness, duplicating rapidly and differentiating itself into a new image. When nothing imposes on the individual, is he really an individual? Only when he thinks so is he determined by the group. In the individual's thoughts and feelings, society lives and breathes as him.

When Bill and Jeff do not depend on society for their sense of who they are, they can affect change in their personal addictions and then in the collective social structures that accommodate steroid and alcohol dependence. Such social structures that exploit individuals reflect consciousness that depends on something it thinks it needs and will do anything for. Social structure changes when we change our relationship to it. The revolution, the reform, is within oneself.

GLOSSARY

affirmation Feeling ontologically secure in the world by achieving the approval of society; feeling secure solely by meeting society's standards of values and competence.

confirmation Feeling ontologically secure in the world prior to society's verification of self-importance.

desocialization The development in self-consciousness of a self separate from society; self-detachment, disinterestedness; vertical change in the perception of oneself in society.

horizontal change Changing one social role for another rather than our attachment to any social role.

levels of social change Individual versus group sources of change in social structure.

resocialization Changing attachment from one social role to another (for example, "If I'm not a sanitation engineer, I'll sell brownies on the corner") in contrast to changing one's attachment to any social role.

social change, principle of Changes in the group's rules for social interaction.

social movement Forms of collective organization (four types: regressive, reform, revolutionary, and utopian) that result in changes in society's prescriptions and proscriptions for behavior.

vertical change Changing one's perception of self in the group as opposed to changing one's self or society.

NOTES

1. Reprinted with permission of the author.
2. Reprinted with permission of the author.
3. This section is based on Lynn M. Mulkey, *Sociology of Education: Theoretical and Empirical Investigations* (Orlando, FL: Harcourt Brace Jovanovich, 1993), pp. 220–222 and 228–229.
4. Quoted from Mulkey, p. 220.
5. Consult the following: Pitirim Sorokin, *Social and Cultural Dynamics* (New York: American Book, 1937); Auguste Comte, *The Positive Philosophy* (New York: AMS Press, 1974); Karl Marx, *Capital: A Critique of Political Economy,* vol. 1 (New York: Random House, 1977; originally published in 1864); Max Weber, *Max Weber: Essays in Sociology,* edited by H. H. Gerth and C. Wright Mills (New York: Oxford University Press, 1946); and Talcott Parsons, *Societies: Evolutionary and Comparative Perspectives* (Englewood Cliffs, NJ: Prentice Hall, 1966).

PART II

UNSEEING SOCIAL STRUCTURE
Being Fully Human through Cooperation

*P*art II of this book is about the second and developmentally significant role of sociology. This part conveys sociology as an idea that facilitates human development through fostering in individuals a realization of the limits of social identity and the relevance of grounding identity outside of society.

Part I of this book introduced a cognitive, conceptual tool that makes sociology a disciplined understanding—how to focus on one aspect of reality, the social aspect. This social aspect refers to how our behavior is continually determined by other people, in one way or another.

In Part I, we also considered six major principles of how others influence our behavior as well as how sociologists explain the operation or nature of these principles through many theories, or sociologies. Thus, in sociology, knowledge of those conditions apart from the individual—the properties of the groups of which individuals are members—influences the behaviors of those individuals. In fact, those behaviors become internalized by individuals so that collectively they

91

exhibit reciprocally the recognizable properties of a group. Part I also illustrated that we observe social forces scientifically by the inclusion of theoretical and empirical investigations relevant to each sociological principle.

Part II discusses the second role of sociology as an idea that facilitates a new awareness in individuals about the limits of the social self and the grounding of identity outside of society. Chapter 8, "Personal Freedom from Social Determinism: Being in Society but Not of It," defines the term *individual freedom.* Chapter 9, "You've Got the Whole World in Your Hands: Changing the Individual, Not Society," discusses how society becomes the object of social change initiated by individual subjects. It presents the ideal society as a product of change in the individual's capacity to see social structure. Chapter 10, "Sociology: Ageless and Always New," is an overview of the significance of sociology.

8

PERSONAL FREEDOM FROM SOCIAL DETERMINISM
Being in Society but Not of It

◆ DISIDENTIFICATION FROM SOCIAL ROLES:
BEYOND MOTHER, FATHER, SISTER, BROTHER

Berdyaev Says, "I Am, Therefore I Think"
and Descartes Says, "I Think, Therefore I Am"

Rain Man: Idiocy and Genius

Plato: Recognition and Cognition

◆ IMPOSTORS FROM OUR SOCIAL PAST

Maurice Sendak's *Where the Wild Things Are*

Viktor Frankl Loses Himself

◆ REALIZATION, NOT EXPLORATION

Excursus from Scholars

"Being in or Beside Oneself": An Excursus by
José Ortega y Gassett

Hesse's *Siddhartha*

Debunking Freud's Debunking:
Reality Is Being Infatuated with Society

*M*eet Maria:

*Why is it that I, when considering my future partner, never realized
before this sociology class that I expect that he will make an equal
or greater amount of money than me, will have an equal or greater
amount of education than me, will have an equal or greater profes-
sional success than me, will have an equal or greater amount of
intelligence than me, and will have an equal or greater ability to
handle things than me?*

The event that made me realize that I have those expectations occurred just two or three weeks ago when I dated a good-looking, nice, 24-year-old guy who seemed to want a serious girlfriend. I didn't really know why, after I dated him, I didn't like him. To help me figure it out, I wondered what it would take to make me accept him more. He would be more acceptable to me if he had a good job instead of driving a truck for an environmental company, if he had a college degree, and things like that. I have high expectations for myself and my future partner, and because most males who I know who are potential future partners have a much lower set of expectations for themselves and their future partners, I wonder if, where, when, and how I will ever find a future partner who meets my expectations of him. I pray that he is out there somewhere![1]

Meet Laura:

I never had any problems interacting with males. Growing up, my father was good to me. He was kind and fair and encouraging. I had friends who were boys throughout my school years. They didn't scare me or intimidate me. Then, as a freshman in college, December 7, 1989, I was raped by a male I had been dating for a short time.

After that, I had reason to be afraid. Men became something different to me that afternoon. They were bigger and stronger. They thought they knew what I needed and wanted. They were selfish. My friends were different, too. They thought I was a liar or a tease. . . .

What happened to me was date rape. Date rape is a product of social prescriptions for how men and women should interact with one another. Men are socialized to be sexual aggressors, and women are socialized to be passive targets. This socialization leads to the stratification among men and women. The man's needs and wants become prominent in the dating situation. The woman's needs are irrelevant or worse, unknown to the woman herself. These sex role perceptions and expectations determine how acquaintance rapes occur because of the changing expectations of men and women in sexual situations.[2]

Both Maria and Laura evidence that their happiness and peace of mind depend on certain social conditions, but in being concerned about the proper acknowledgment of their social selves, they impede the very fulfillment of that which they think they need. In not needing what they think they need, are they better able to fulfill their social nature? They can come to accept their social destiny but not depend on it for their security. They can make fair and equitable values that are human because they do not need them for their sense of well-being.

The ego, or social self, orients itself to having and getting. Its attention is on weight, hair, sex appeal, the right partner, and the right treatment in matters of sexual expression. While important, these social features leave out the reality of true identity. By obsessing with these qualities as means rather than as ends in our perception makes us afraid that we're not good enough, afraid we'll be losing or lacking something in life. Only upon realizing that we are none of these things and that *being* is the sole determinant of our value are we better able to do what we need to.

We relinquish our attachment to any form of expression of ourselves. For example, in some societies, elders are regarded with respect and honor. But in American society (or our personality as society), an aged body makes us feel like a worthless person. Being young is better, only because we think so as part of our collective personal judgment.

Changing our minds so that we are free and not determined—so that society is in us and we are not in it—means deferring our social selves to a greater vision, one that sees the world as the opportunity for offering ourselves, not getting for the self. Then, at the moment when we do not need to be affirmed by society in some or any way, we will be able to act in a situation without self-centeredness; we will be free emotionally to be ourselves because we will not be preoccupied with social self-defense. The elderly person, in recognizing feelings of worthlessness as society's judgment, can now decide what to do with it rather than react automatically to it. Maria, for example, recognizes the sources of her attractions, but whether they are fulfilled does not determine her sense of happiness. This doesn't mean that Maria should not have an appropriate partner or that Laura should not be treated sexually against her will. It means that Maria and Laura are not diminished in their sense of who they are when a form of relatedness is not what they expect. They are then best able to act in the matter.

*S*ociology's second role is as an idea that facilitates a new awareness in individuals about the limits of the social self and the grounding of identity outside society. In this role, sociology documents all the ways in which we are determined by society so that we can finally ask, Well, then, what is it to be individual? In this role, sociology locates for us that place in ourselves that was lost to our awareness, temporarily, and in that way makes possible the experience of individual freedom from social determinism. Society is revealed to be a point in human development, an attachment, even an addiction initially. It's something we might think we need, and when we are worried about getting the next "fix," we are never free to *be* instead of *do*.

The great and essential insights of sociology are its disclosure of two ways, or perceptions, of being in the world. Sociology makes available the social nature of what we are and shows us the two ways in which our social nature operates: We are first attached to it, until we come to express through it; *attachment* is the very occasion to develop *expression*. Each awareness of ourselves (as society or in but not of it) has relevance for our individual well-being and that of society. For example, countless women feel that they are less than whole and happy humans because they haven't borne children. These women *are* only when they *equal* society. Maria and Laura experience personal pain because they react to society—to their personalities—as if that is solely what they are. They experience themselves as female humans rather than as human females.

We have come to see social structure, or that society is the us we first come to know as ourselves. This is human sociality, the method of cooperation. Its consequences, however, are that we expend ourselves in defense of our social selves and that society and its rules reflect the regulation of self-interest rather than the grace that subsumes the law by accepting others for who they really are. The social self divides us, but our true self sees itself as every person. The ego interferes with the clear expression of who we are by trying to get us to add to it or to take something away from it. We don't call up to consciousness the sense of the self actually doing these things.

DISIDENTIFICATION FROM SOCIAL ROLES: BEYOND MOTHER, FATHER, SISTER, BROTHER

It's one thing to talk about personal freedom from social determinism but another to achieve it. All the talk in the world about what it takes to be a gymnast will not make one. I must turn within to the discipline of practicing the principles of sociology's second essential insight: *disidentification* with society—*unseeing* social structure.

Berdyaev Says, "I Am, Therefore I Think" and Descartes Says, "I Think, Therefore I Am"

Unseeing means shifting one's self-awareness from the philosophical and Descartean notion of an I doing the thinking to the social philosopher Nickolai Berdyaev's notion of experiencing the thinking as the I.[3] Finding oneself is an exercise in the return to "the before the once seen," as noted by Ludwig Wittgenstein, an early twentieth-century Austrian philosopher.[4] We haven't really seen the world before. What we see and respond to is our learned attention to and judgment of the world. "Pay attention to pimples—they are bad. Encourage them, discourage them; people with pimples are bad." When we are able to experience or be aware of the world without judging it, that is "the before the once seen."

To observe our social determinism is the "practice school of sociology," a process of learning beyond what we already know.[5] In other words, we come to see that social thought and the thinker are really one; the *I feel* is transformed to the *feeling is I*. The everydayness of the world is replaced with the feeling that the world is a strange place.

To be free is not to change the world but to change our awareness of our relationship to it. The displacement of attention from social self to self-awareness is a routine activity, a discipline, a sensitivity to the world available exclusively through active exercise in beholding the mind. For example, in an exercise for defamiliarizing ourselves with what we already know as real, Bernard McGrane[6] prescribes stopping during one meal to observe what is on the plate for three minutes before beginning to eat; the instructions also include eating without utensils, just hands. The felt naturalness and palatability of fried chicken shifts to the awareness of the chicken as a dead animal. The distinction attained in consciousness between the naturalness of the fried chicken and the chicken as a dead animal fosters another perception: the self before any social concept impinges on its experience.

Here is another example of achieving freedom in contrast to talking about it: I love Irish creme coffee, but I lose the awareness of its taste when I am mindful of what I am going to do at 10:00 A.M. or 3:00 P.M. today. Will I make it to the meeting on time? Will I have time to swim? Did so and so like what I was wearing? Whenever any thought takes me away from tasting the coffee, I let go of it and return to the taste of the coffee. Eventually, the distraction of thought is replaced with sheer awareness—being as opposed to doing.

In this state of awareness, I do not react to nor am I determined by anything because every emotional response and behavior is actually a reaction to my mind, a concept of the world, and concepts become separate in my mind when I watch them. My attachment is broken, and the experience of being replaces the automatic, unthinking reaction to everyone and everything I am thinking about. Social self-awareness is necessary for the attainment of freedom; the natural attitude must be bracketed.[7] The discipline of mind—of unknowing, so to speak—produces a facility of sensitivity to the ground of being of everyday experience. The felt shift in identification and attachment from the social to the ground of experience transforms our understanding of the relation of principles and theories of sociology from an explanation of the determinants of our behavior to an expression of them. I am not these things. Now, what do I do with them, based on the recognition that I *am* before I *do* anything.

Rain Man: Idiocy and Genius

When we reach that state when we no longer automatically look at people and things in terms of, Are they good for me? Bad for me? and so on, we can then use every social interaction as an avenue for the expression of the intrinsic value of our being—the being that doesn't need any more so it gives of itself. In the movie *Rain Man*, Dustin Hoffman shows through his character, Raymond, that neither idiocy nor genius matter. At the social level, they matter in terms of our instrumental mentality, but at the transcendent level of our self-awareness, both are chances for giving.

Plato: Recognition and Cognition

Plato makes the distinction between *cognition*—our instrumental way of getting around in the world—and another way made available through *recognition,* a return to what makes cognition possible. We know about ourselves before we know ourselves. The self was there all the time, and we did not know it. Every so-called problem, every so-called need is an opportunity for development into the full stature of our being, our individual nature.

◆ IMPOSTORS FROM OUR SOCIAL PAST

Once we rest in the feeling that we *are* before we *become,* then impostors from our social past surface to immediate awareness. We can let go of them emotionally by saying to ourselves that we are not really those things. There is no past except in how we use it as memory to inform the present, and the present is a new standard, or evaluation. On the one hand, memory is an added, adaptive feature because it provides us with broad alternatives in how to see ourselves in the world; on the other hand, we tend to accept these voices of the past, telling us who we are, as authoritative in our present experience. We can be free from the social determinism of the past simply by recognizing it.

Maurice Sendak's *Where the Wild Things Are*

In his book *Where the Wild Things Are*, Maurice Sendak[8] describes how the boy Max stared into the eyes of the beasts, unafraid, empowered by facing them. What scares us from the past is real because we bring it into the present. This is a lesson of self-reflection that teaches us to recognize our social self-identification. Being is perceptible when we let go of our thoughts or anything else that tells us who we are.

Viktor Frankl Loses Himself

Our experiences in life—however we refer to them, good or bad—are lessons in the knowledge of who we are. In its first essential insight, sociology shows us what we think we are, so that it brings us, via its second essential insight, to that place in our awareness of who we are.

In the lesson of having been a survivor of the German concentration camps, Viktor Frankl[9] lost all of himself by societal standards. He lost his roles, his familiar ways of being a human, his social arena. In losing the person he thought was himself, he found what had been there all along but lost in another awareness of himself.

REALIZATION, NOT EXPLORATION

We act as if we matter as persons, subject to our understanding of ourselves—the rational, instrumental, social, utilitarian idea of ourselves—when actually, we never find ourselves through an exploration of ideas. We are ourselves finding, exploring. This is a different kind of awareness; it is an awakening or realization that shifts our orientation from searching to contentment.

Personal freedom from social determinism is the story of sociology. Sociology, as a science, is at the same time a step or stage in human development. It permits a shift in what psychologist Abraham Maslow[10] called *being cognition*—not a magical transformation but a transformation of everything into the magical. Maslow says we experience an *intrinsic conscience* beyond the superego. In other words, we do not *seek* to find ourselves; we simply experience a new awareness of ourselves. In that we are anchored, with new intentions and under a new auspices, to employ the varied social forms for the expression of our selves, as opposed to finding ourselves.

Excursus from Scholars

Sociology has given most of its energies to its first essential insight.[11] In its investigation of the relationship of the individual to the group, it makes available the causes and consequences of the human's identification with her socially assigned identities. Peter Berger, in *Invitation to Sociology: A Humanistic Perspective,*[12] is one of several scholars who reminds us of sociology's second essential insight: The socialized human forgets her fundamental nature, the one that sponsors the development of the social self. This sense of being human stands behind being racist or liberal or any category of instruction for human relatedness and asks whether either or neither category is how we want to express the intrinsic value of just being. Berger admonishes us that the human knows herself according to the fragmented categories of learned ways of feeling and acting; the intrinsic worth of being a person is disguised in its consciousness as a social role. The human forgets that she has invented what is now an automatic response. The individual is a person who can distinguish herself from herself as social role. This realization, sociology's second essential insight—unseeing—is a step in the development of the full stature of being human.

In another of his works, *The Sacred Canopy,*[13] Berger distinguishes scientific and transcendent states of consciousness. He says that consciousness is antecedent to socialization and that it can never be totally socialized; it is always partial. A part of consciousness is styled by socialization into a form known as a person's *personality*. The social self is a set of representations of rules for human cooperation that becomes alienated from the consciousness upon which it has been imposed.

The Hidden Injuries of Class is a sociological analysis by Richard Sennett and Jonathan Cobb,[14] who highlight sociology's two essential insights: Individual development progresses from social scientific understanding of the social self to a transcendent awareness of self. They note that people change "horizontally" from one set of learned behaviors to another but leave their relationships to social role unchanged.[15] At this level of human understanding, people risk annihilation of their dignity and self-definition. Sennett and Cobb further note that personal consciousness can be more than a "storage locker" for social information and that the human consciousness allows the individual to rearrange the information society furnishes for social self-development. This rearrangement results in a division of the self in terms of the *real* person and the *performing* person and fosters the transcendence of pain a person would otherwise experience if she had to submit the whole of herself to the group.

The theme of sociology's second insight is further noted in a discussion of how the ontologically secure person has an inner capacity that is greater than her tangible works. This person experiences an innate sense of wholeness and integration and can therefore master every situation without being attached to any. She may deviate or conform to social forms according to a new standard of disinterestedness that replaces defensive social selfishness.[16]

Roberto Assagioli,[17] a medical doctor and psychologist, claims that the normal mistake all people make is to identify with some *content* of consciousness rather than with consciousness itself. Some people, he explains, get their identities from their feelings; others from their thoughts according to their social roles. But this identification with part of the personality impedes the freedom that comes from the experience of the pure *I*. Assagioli distinguishes identification with the *predicate* as opposed to the *subject*. Often, a crisis removes from a person the role with which she identifies: a runner permanently injures her leg, a wife betrays her spouse, a committed employee loses her job. Disidentification is forced on the individual, and the person enters into a fuller identity. This exercise in disidentification involves affirming: "I have a body, but I am not my body; I have feelings, but I am not my feelings; I have a job, but I am not my job." Systematic introspection can help diminish all partial self-identifications. This leads to the experience of the observer being different from what she observes. She recognizes and affirms: "I am fundamentally self-consciousness, which wills, directs, and employs all my psychological and physical capabilities in its service."

In the tradition of Maslow's[18] "farther reaches of human experience," Lawrence LeShan[19] distinguishes between scientific and transcendent perceptions of reality. One way of comprehending reality is not superior to the other. Rather, for the fullest humanhood, a person needs both. LeShan refers to the Roman mystic Plotinus, who said the human being must be seen as an amphibian who needs both life on land and life in the water to achieve fullest amphibianhood. Likewise, humans need to be at home in the world in two different states of consciousness for complete development.

Bertrand Russell's[20] ideas convey and confirm the sociological significance of the distinction between *scientific* and *transcendent* realities.[21] Russell states that humans have a habit of thinking in the direction of service to the self. Everything is given fragmentary consideration; we view things as means to help or hinder our own purposes. Some persons come to experience a more unified world than that of conventional social belief, where imperfection is integrated by a contemplation that bestows worth of the whole of experience. This quality of infinity is simply another way of regarding the same objects.

"Being in or Beside Oneself": An Excursus by José Ortega y Gassett

To be beside oneself, says José Ortega y Gassett,[22] is the estrangement in self-awareness that we are separate from the one thinking so. Being in oneself is the restoration in awareness of viewing oneself. This self experiences itself as the basis of all social expression and is achieved by mental disidentification with social definitions.

Hesse's *Siddhartha*

Hermann Hesse[23] distinguishes *being as seeking itself* from *being itself* in the characters Govinda and Siddhartha. Govinda leaves the planet, never realizing that he cannot find himself by understanding. Siddhartha realizes that the understanding is already an attribute of who he is. Hesse's other work emphasizes how the mode of understanding oneself to find self, represented by Govinda, is a process of self-objectification that presumes a rational or instrumental orientation of subjectivity in contrast to a selfless orientation of transcendent consciousness.

> *Only when our gaze becomes pure consciousness, does the Self open itself to us; if I inspect a forest with the intention of buying it, renting it, cutting it down, going hunting in it, or mortgaging it, then I do not see the forest but only its relation to my desires, plans, and concerns, to my purse. Then it consists of wood, it is young or old, healthy or diseased. But if I want nothing from it but to gaze thoughtlessly, into its green depths, then it becomes a forest, nature, a growing thing; only then is it beautiful. At the moment when desire ceases and contemplation, pure seeing, and self-surrender begin, everything changes. We cease to be useful or dangerous, interesting or boring, genial or rude, strong or weak. We become nature, we become beautiful and remarkable as does everything that is an object of clear contemplation. For indeed contemplation is not scrutiny or criticism, it is nothing but love. It is the highest and most desirable state of being; undemanding love.[24]*

Debunking Freud's Debunking: Reality Is Being Infatuated with Society

Sigmund Freud's idea that love is an illusion is the opposite of what, for me, is reality. Any reality that permits the bestowal of unconditional regard upon the world is the one I want to experience. When I understand that stars, grass, vomit, pain, and maggots all exist before I judge them, I have experienced the movement from seeing to unseeing. I experience myself without trying to make myself experience, and in this, I debunk the *myth* of social determinism to find the *reality* of personal freedom.

This chapter has focused on the practice of sociology's insight— disidentification—on breaking our identifications with our social roles. The practice means seeing social structure in its many forms, especially from our past, as the opportunity to realize we *are* already; there is nothing to find or defend.

In the name of this focus on the practice of sociology's second insight, we have encountered the achievement of social awareness as a precondition for the development of transcendent awareness and individual freedom referred to or interpreted in the selected works of other scholars. The next chapter draws on the works of others to emphasize and to further interpret the shift in our awareness of our selves as society to society in us and to clarify what sociology offers as tools for seeing and unseeing social structure.

GLOSSARY

cognition   The social self experienced via the mind; the consciousness of oneself as socially, instrumentally valued.
disidentification   Emotional detachment or self-security experienced separately from the social role.
exploration   A search for self through understanding or through rational ideas and/or beliefs.
realization   Expanded, enhanced development and differentiation in self-awareness and consciousness of reality.
recognition   A return to the perceived sense of self prior to the self known via the mind (as social role).

NOTES

1. Reprinted with permission of the author.
2. Reprinted with permission of the author.
3. Nickolai Berdyaev, *Slavery and Freedom* (New York: Charles Scribner's Sons, 1944); and René Descartes, *Le Discourse de la Méthode* (1637).
4. Ludwig Wittgenstein, *Philosophical Investigations* (New York: Basil Blackwell, 1958).
5. Bernard McGrane, *Society, Self and De-Socialization* (Orange, CA: Chapman University, Sociology Department, 1991).

6. Here are two accounts of watching the mind (from McGrane):
   Case 1—*After staring at my dinner for three minutes, I became nauseous over the thought of eating fried chicken. I couldn't touch it and proceeded to eat my vegetables, roll, and salad with my hands. Different thoughts came to my head, and I found myself thinking about a chicken, running around a yard, eating seeds. The thought of eating an animal that was once alive repulsed me. A dead animal was sitting on my plate. Well, what am I really eating? I'm eating an animal that consists of seeds, veins, blood, and bones, and the thought of biting into this was not good. Eating potatoes, salad, and vegetables with my fingers seemed so animalistic. I had to lick my fingers clean every time I took a bite because I hated to feel messy.*

   Case 2—*It's interesting to consider that I don't normally entertain these reflections as I carry on my daily routines. Maybe I should, but I don't. Perhaps if I were more reflective about more of my automatic behaviors, I would have different perspectives about life than I do when I perform so automatically like I am conditioned to do.*

7. A. Schutz, *The Phenomenology of the Social World* (Evanston, IL: Northwestern University Press, 1967).
8. Maurice Sendak, *Where the Wild Things Are* (New York: Harper & Row, 1981).
9. Viktor Frankl, *The Unheard Cry for Meaning: Psychotherapy and Humanism* (New York: Simon and Schuster, 1978).
10. Abraham Maslow, *Toward a Psychology of Being* (Princeton, NJ: Van Nostrand, 1968).
11. This section is based on Lynn M. Mulkey, *Sociology of Education: Theoretical and Empirical Investigations* (Orlando, FL: Harcourt Brace Jovanovich, 1993), pp. xviii–xix.
12. Peter Berger, *Invitation to Sociology: A Humanistic Perspective* (New York: Doubleday, 1963).
13. Peter Berger, *The Sacred Canopy: Elements of a Sociological Theory of Religion* (New York: Doubleday, 1967).
14. Richard Sennett and Jonathan Cobb, *The Hidden Injuries of Class* (New York: Vintage Books, 1972).
15. *Deconstructionist* (postmodernist) (Foucault, *Theory, Culture, and Society* [New York: Pantheon, 1985]) arguments are not about disidentification and transcendence; they illustrate identifying with one social role instead of another.
16. I. Bell, "Buddhist Sociology: Some Thoughts on the Convergence of Sociology and the Eastern Paths of Liberation," in *Theoretical Perspectives in Sociology,* ed. Scott G. McNall (New York: St. Martin's Press, 1979).
17. Roberto Assagioli, *The Act of Will* (New York: Viking Press, 1973).
18. Abraham Maslow, *The Farther Reaches of Human Nature* (New York: Penguin, 1971), p. 327. Also see Deepak Chopra, M.D., *Unconditional Life: Mastering the Forces That Shape Personal Reality* (New York: Harper Collins, 1991).

19. Lawrence LeShan, "The Social Significance of Meditation," in *How to Meditate: A Guide to Self-Discovery* (New York: Bantam Books, 1974).
20. Bertrand Russell, "The Essence of Religion," in *The Basic Writings of Bertrand Russell* (New York: Simon & Schuster, 1961).
21. This section is based on Mulkey, pp. 240–241.
22. José Ortega y Gassett, *Man and People*, trans. Willard R. Trask (New York: W. W. Norton, 1957).
23. Hermann Hesse, *Siddhartha* (New York: Harper & Row, 1965).
24. Hermann Hesse, "Concerning the Soul, 1917," in *My Belief: Essays, 1904–1961, On Life and Art,* ed. and introduction by Theodore Ziolkowski, trans. Denver Lindley and Ralph Manheim (New York: Farrar, Straus and Giroux, 1976).

9 YOU'VE GOT THE WHOLE WORLD IN YOUR HANDS
Changing the Individual, Not Society

◆ SOCIETY AS OBJECT AND YOU AS SUBJECT

Josiah Royce and Society as the Community of Love

Joseph Campbell's Hero in Society

◆ PRESERVING SELFLESSNESS

Janis Joplin: "Freedom's Just Another Word for Nothin' Left to Lose"

Finding Yourself in the Normal Distribution and the *New York Times* Weekend Section

Merleau-Ponty on Prereflective Self

*M*eet me.

The Center for Teaching Excellence at my university invited me to give a lecture. I accepted the invitation and was introduced by a sponsor who presented a glowing review of my credentials. When I got to the microphone, I said to the audience that I wanted them to know something about me that is perhaps a better credential for my expertise than what had been identified about me. My best credentials, I declared, are the facts that I have a facial scar from the surgical excision of a congenital lymphangioma and that I have a sister, now 44, who is schizophrenic and has been living in a mental institution since she was 16.

I said that my credentials—I mean that, for me, the conventional ways for feeling secure in the world, knowing how and when people will respond to me and I to them in a predictable way so I can feel in control of getting my needs met—were not available and seemingly sabotaged. My Ph.D., in fact, was at one time just a compensation, an alternatively acceptable way for me to get the approval of others in such a way that I followed the collective road map for living. Now, however, it has become transformed as an instrument for me to further understand what are the causes and consequences of my being a self.

My insidious cancer and my crazy sister have been, accidentally and paradoxically, the very occasions whereby I've come to understand and experience new aspects of what it is to be human. They have been the very invitations to finding, as might an athlete, the farthest reaches of human development not found through normal vision but rather through the cultivation of a process, a discipline, available to but not realized by all. I have been preoccupied with the question of what it is to be human and about the influence other people have on my behavior, on me, on what a me is in the first place.

For example, I used to think, like might most of us Americans, that when I ride the subway in Manhattan and the person across from me is picking his nose, it is my disgust—naturally so, inherently so—that I'm feeling. It belongs to me, it is my feeling, my emotion, my personality that is oriented toward the other person as disgust. Or, for instance, I know now that my disgust for the woman on the bus who had hairy legs belonged first to society—the United States, the group—and became me, my personality. I have pondered my relationship to the group, others, and discovered that I'm not who I thought I was.

I have learned there are two ways in which to be a self, an individual, each with different consequences for me and for people around me. Moreover, one self is determined by society—in fact, is society—and a slave to society, always nervously monitoring whether it is what society expects. It is the self that is the stockbroker who jumps out the window when the market crashes. It is the self who is the 50-year-old woman who regains her lost sense of self defined by her sexuality by having breast implants, a facelift, and liposuction.

The second way to be a self is free from society yet simultaneously stable and anchored in the world—in it but not of it. The second self is an adaptation of the first and, in fact, is possible as a sequel to and contingent on the first way of being a self. In my attempt to survive, I stumbled onto the resources for a different self-construction. This book is an account, an intellectual rendering, a sociological interpretation of this, my human experience.

I learned that to be human is to be "aware" of being human. The human capacity to be itself by being aware of it as a self is a phenomenon (an adaptive feature of the human organism) that is possible because the human can experience itself as both an I, a subject, and a me, an object of a subject. The self is not a given but emergent through a succession of joint enterprises with others, enterprises made possible via the mind and society. The mind consolidates the group's rules, society's rules, about how to go about feeling and acting in relation to other people and things. Society, the rules, becomes embodied, via the mind, as personality, not in personality.

The I is the basis for two self-awarenesses: the self as the object of itself and the self as the transcendence of itself as object. The I, Lynn, can be either aware of herself as the "talker" (or in other words, identified or equated with society's definition of who she is) or aware of herself as expressing herself through society's definition (the "talker") of who she is. The trust is in the source, not in what it represents.

Thus, we're not who we think we are. But we must first see what we think we are, and then we can manifest the fullness of our development. We are far away from ourselves.

*I*t boils down to one precipitate: Society can become the object of social change via change in the individual's perception of who he is in relation to it. The ideal society is a product of change in a person's capacity to see social structure. The first self believes what it sees; the second self is the one who unsees by sensing the *it* that is seeing in the first place. This second self-perception transforms or changes the world by changing its perception of the world.

SOCIETY AS OBJECT AND YOU AS SUBJECT

For example, in the nail shop, my "fingist," as I refer to her, is Korean. When I no longer *feel different*—that I am American and she is Korean—and instead *recognize difference* but feel we are one or alike in our essential humanity, then I am in a state of awareness that makes society not a defense of difference but a provision for it. I am disidentifying with the meaning of myself as American. Only then am I beyond a basis for my feelings and actions—that I am this and she is that—and only then am I the subject rather than determined by society in my sense of who I am.

Let me emphasize that the feeling that I am distinct and separate from another person is what gets in my way. Identity grounded simply in being is unseeing social structure and returning to the difference as social structure for the occasion, the expression of giving and not a defense of being.

We can imagine now, sociologically, that being a subject requires seeing the obvious and beyond it. Imagine that the ultimate form of human evolutionary adaptation is the human's capacity for having by *giving* rather than having by *getting*. It isn't that we won't have, but worrying about having is the radical point of our personal and societal problems. This new contemplation is an infatuation with the world. Everything takes on a new meaning beyond the instrumental. Work becomes fun, and home becomes work. The attitude of everydayness is *mine* and *theirs, me* and *them, I* and *you*.

But this awareness is a false sense of proprietorship; the claim to owning is as silly as the claim to sunshine, to vision, to having a heartbeat. We don't own anything, really, so there's nothing to get. We leave our notion of *mine* and return to it as an expression, not a possession. Will and emotion are under new direction. Sociology seems to tell us we're coded, developmentally, for two ways of being: fearful to peaceful. I do not change the world but my feeling about it. When I am not fearing, I automatically make decisions in behalf of others. To change the world by changing my view of it is what sociology is about. Sociology reveals it scientifically as part of our consciousness and, in that, moves us to the possibility for a greater experience of self in society. And then sociology studies society again.

It may seem difficult to change our usual way of being aware of who we are. Every time I see somebody or something, I immediately think of it in terms of how it's good for me, not me for it. The challenge of living in the world lies in changing my view of it. It's not easy. At the gym, I recognize the feeling of the *me* in a young man's face—I'm tough; my toughness is me. If toughness is the *me,* then the world is a place in which to defend gym equipment and things that place a value on being tough.

The evolution of cooperation is the resolution to find completeness in oneself. But this is a lesson learned through our very attachment to our social selves. To see that self is to see what we don't need, at least in the same way.

Here is an additional comment on the detail of how the realization of society as object is premised on our seeing social structure (society) as subject. (This discussion supplements the introduction to becoming a personality via society in Chapter 2 on socialization.) On public television, I saw a cheetah eating the guts of a gazelle while the gazelle was still alive. The cheetah is programmed genetically to be directly dependent on its environment for its survival.

Basically, the human seems adaptive in his ability to defer his reliance on the environment for survival by way of constructing self-awareness. He responds not to mother's milk but to the words "It's Mother. I'll be there soon." The human has the capacity to construct two selves—a social self and a direct awareness of self—each with specific relevance for the human and everyone together. These are fundamentally two degrees, or levels, of deference of the organism to impulse. One self is oriented to self-preservation, less than in the cheetah's; the other self is self-preserving but by self-giving. The first self-construction produces the social nature of the organism, the deference of impulse to the rules of the group; the second self-construction perfects the social nature so that the consequence for the individual is enhanced self-determination, freedom, and fulfillment and the possibility of the ideal society, a community of self-disinterest.

This process begins with socialization, or the relation of mind to society in the formation of the self as an object to itself. The human organism is neither inherently human nor does he find his humanity in the environment, society. Rather, it is through the interaction of mind and society that the human comes to know himself as a self. The human *depends on* (is determined by) the group, the collective, the society, for instructions on how to feel and act. This is the *transactional* view of the self.[1] The behavior of the individual can be understood in terms of the behavior of the whole social group (society). Society exists as a set of prescriptions, transmitted from one generation to the next, beyond the life of each of its members. This beyondness of society is important for our understanding of individual behavior because it reveals the importance of the *I's* capacity to be aware of itself beyond society.

Part I showed us that personality is society embodied *as* the individual, not *in* the individual. Each individual is a note in a symphony. Each, seemingly unique, is understood in light of the whole. As stated earlier in this book, the gill on the fish is understandable only in the context of the ocean. Similarly, personality is understood in light of society. Personality is the embodiment of society as a set of individual directives encoded as personality. The relations valued by the group are encoded as properties of the brain (cognition, will, emotion, sensory experience) so that the "out there" is a standard, a context for the development of self-awareness—the self "out there," in and as the group.

For example, it is hard to believe that being a mother isn't a natural part of being a female, but the so-called maternal instinct (the unconditional regard of the biological mother for her offspring) is invalid. Contrary to my mother saying that there is a natural and inherent bond between us is the reality that *mother* is another word that belongs to society first. Society says, "Take this amorphous protoplasm, call it *mother*, and tell her she will regard her biological offspring unconditionally, by fulfilling a given set of obligations." Society says to take this person, the biological parent, when it could be another person off the street. Fathers can bond with infants just as mothers can. The literature on adopted children also testifies to the social definition of *mother*. The degree to which we become competent in what society expects (in this case, being a mother) is the social self, and how well society becomes personality is measured by our sense of self-worth, or self-esteem.

If we need society to develop social self-awareness, then we are determined by society in our sense of self. The hallmark of human adaptive capability is the capacity to retain self-worth that does not depend on society for material or social affirmation. It is the development in our self-awareness that we cannot lose what we never had in the first place. Two self-perceptions are available to us: social self-awareness and direct awareness of self, "I think, therefore I am" or "I am, therefore I think." This second awareness is the felt realization in every moment of the distinction between the subject precursory to itself, antecedent of a personality. It is an awareness of an *I* disidentified from or transcendent of the experience of the *me* (the socially recognized self). It is the residual presence of oneself when all ideas of self are dismissed.

I want to add even more detail on what is important to the sociologist about this process of society as subject and self-construction. Why does it happen, and how does it happen? The human, through the objectification of thoughts and feelings, survives by way of his ability to defer his impulses to the rules of the group and thereby make social order possible. The human also has the potential to subordinate even his social impulses to the control of transcendent, direct self-awareness. Other organisms depend on the modification of their genes to adjust to environmental conditions. Humans are able to construct different selves as a way of meeting life's challenges.

The human responds not to the environment but to the *meaning* he assigns to the environment. The epitome of human adaptation is an evolutionary feature called *self-awareness* that can yield a self that is self-defensive or another that is self-complete. Ultimately and profoundly, the human has the capacity of being a self that can retain itself as self, despite the environment, not because of it.

Let me go on further with this discussion of what it means to be a *subject in* versus an *object of* society. This is part of the sociologist's expertise in understanding the relation of the individual to other people. Self-objectification (you'll recall from Chapter 2 on socialization), in the name of adaptation, is the process that involves the self as an object to itself. For example, it is the ability for reflexivity; the individual holding the attitude (the *I*) and the object toward whom the attitude is held (the *me*) are the same person.[2] These are two distinct forms of consciousness, or awareness. The individual (or *I* awareness) is aware of itself thinking and feeling. The I, via the instrument of the mind (brain), keeps itself under constant vigilance. The I, for example, reflects on itself as a person disgusted with women who don't shave their legs.

The I's reflection on itself as a me is a development in self-awareness. This self develops slowly from birth. Different features of the self come to be objectified in the course of development. The child becomes aware of himself as an ego by taking on the attitudes of others and experiencing (thinking and feeling) how others feel and think about him. There is no self apart from society. Society is a set of rules that exists beyond the lives of individuals; the rules are transmitted and achieved in the individual as the embodiment of society (personality) or the encoding in mind of the mutual orientations of individuals toward each other. Society is the internalized attitudes of the community as a whole—the system of attitudes, values, and conceptions of right and wrong behavior. Other animals do not defer action until they decide about what to feel and what to do with their biology—to manage hunger by going on a fast, for example.

Each self is somewhat unique as a result of the peculiar combination of the attitudes of others, yet the response of the organism to the attitudes of others is a universal, uniform phenomenon. Every human recognizes himself as a set of learned orientations to others in the group of which he is a member.

We must know which status to assume, when, where, and how: What am I now, in this situation or as this situation? Am I a fat person, an uncle, an American, or what? Self-esteem is a barometer for a person's skill, talent, and knowledgeable role performance upon which society depends. The human brings the capacity for social self-construction, and in this way, society provides the ways in which he can become a self. The social self experiences itself as a consolidation of directions, of external and internalized moral and behavioral dictates.

This self becomes the very basis of a second, sequel self-construction—the social self devoid of all concept of itself.

Josiah Royce and Society as the Community of Love

Now putting aside this rather lengthy talk about the development of society as object and we are the subjects, we will consider how being a subject has consequences for the structure of society. The second capacity for self-construction releases the human from identification with the world and replaces it with identification with the ground of being. In this mode of self-awareness, the human exhibits the optimum degree of adaptation because he can sustain a sense of himself despite any external, material, or social threat. The kind of self-construction is a continual practice, a discipline of vertical change—not change in the part one plays in society but ongoing change in the *relationship* to the part one plays in society.

This vertical change is desocialization, the conscious act of the I saying to every social situation, I am but not this. This self acts itself *through* society but not *as* it. This self makes society an ideal community, as Josiah Royce,[3] an American philosopher, would say, in contrast to a place, a society, or social structure of relatedness for getting and maintaining oneself. People work to give and get for giving.

Joseph Campbell's Hero in Society

Author Joseph Campbell[4] says the hero is one who can walk through the fire and not be burned because he sees that society is a transparency for the radiance of the self, rather than the sole source of the self. Campbell says that, for the most part, sociology has emphasized the view of persons as dependent on society for who they are and what they do. The individual is solely a social self—a social construction and a necessary construction, one without which the individual cannot function—and this social self operates on the basis of self-preservation and self-interest. Even the relativity and apparent indeterminateness of cultural definitions for self, in the final word, return the individual to his dependence on the group to find himself. While the culture of the group is the rich cultural heritage needed to enable the individual to find himself, the logical dilemma here is that there is no freedom or self-governance for a being that depends on external affirmation of itself, for a self that is constantly oriented to sustaining itself.

PRESERVING SELFLESSNESS

Well, here we are, close to the end of the story where self-preservation becomes a preservation of selflessness. What it means to be an individual is found at the end of a developmental sequence in consciousness; self-awareness is experienced as an alternate line of reality.[5]

> *Our evaluation of happiness and unhappiness is bound with a motion along an envisioned line leading to a desired end. In the fulfillment of this*

course of means to end, not in the fulfillment of the self as point do we find value. Our conception of freedom rests on the principles of noninterference with this moving line, noninterruption of the intended course of action. Our conception of self (personality) formation, our stress on the significance of success and failure and of frustration in general, is grounded in the axiomatically postulated line. If I walk along a path because I like the country, or if it is not important to get to a particular point at a particular time, then the insuperable puddle from the morning's shower is not frustrating; I throw stones into it and watch the ripples, and then choose another path. If the undertaking is of value in itself, a point good in itself, and not because it leads to something, then failure has no symbolic meaning; it merely results in no cake for supper, or less money in the family budget; it is not personally destructive. But failure is devastating in our culture because it is not failure of the undertaking alone; it is the moving, becoming, lineally conceived self which has failed.[6]

Janis Joplin: "Freedom's Just Another Word for Nothin' Left to Lose"

In her song "Me and Bobby McGee," Janis Joplin, a 1960s artist, says in her own way what is sociology's second essential insight: "Freedom's just another word for nothin' left to lose." When we don't need ourselves from society, we are no longer determined by it. It isn't that we don't recognize our need for being social in the same manner that we acknowledge our need for oxygen, but when we don't worry about it, the world becomes a better place. In the ideal society, love generates or subsumes the law, those rules that represent cooperation or the taking of others into account. The ideal community becomes manifest when the principles and theories of collective behavior represent disinterest and self-giving rather than the regulation of self-interest. Societal forms are objectifications of various degrees of individual self-realization (totalitarian, democratic, socialistic, communistic regimes). The features of whole societies reflect the developmental level of individual consciousness, externalized and collectively objectified.

The I's consummate role in the development or realization of individual subjectivity is the awareness alienated from perception during the process of the development of the ego, the social self. A part of being human is not socialized or transformed into social identity; this residual state of unsocialized self eventually emerges in individual consciousness, so that persons are freed from identifying totally with their social roles.

Finding Yourself in the Normal Distribution and the *New York Times* Weekend Section

On the average, people are their social selves, but that doesn't mean that one outlier cannot change the normal distribution. We can account only for our own destiny and take responsibility for our own development. Our social selves obstruct our vision of our basic selves that is disguised in our consciousnesses as social roles. When we experience ourselves behind all identities, then we are ourselves.

The liberated individual is one whose identity is not the same as his social role. In our investigation of who we are and to what extent we are associated with others, we typically define the social self as the only self and, in taking this stance, lose sight of the second contribution of I in the development of what is our individuality. The most difficult thing about this development process is the constant discipline in awareness required to invoke it. We are constantly tempted to think that part of our reality is acceptable and part of it is not—some good, some bad—instead of seeing that everything is already together—the good and the bad. We are accustomed to living in a state of alienation, mesmerized and bombarded with stimuli that reinforce our experience of our social selves and its accompanying realm of successes and failures. The *New York Times* weekend section typically harbors themes of the social self—greed, lust, and evil. For example, in one edition,[7] Michiko Kakutani reviewed Patrick McGrath's novel *Dr. Haggard's Disease*, noting that the author "stretches the limits of humans' capacity for evil and perversion." *Someone to Watch Over Me*, a Broadway play nominated for a Tony award, hints at the idea that security is never found within but external to ourselves. And, of course, this is the fiction that is a lesson for our growth to authentic self-reliance.

Merleau-Ponty on Prereflective Self

Maurice Merleau-Ponty, a French philosopher, alludes to basic self-awareness as a *prereflective self*.[8] This is the I, or self-awareness, before it views itself as the object of society. The human capacities for adaptation through cooperation and to affect and perfect society are actualized when the person comes to see society as a context for the development of his very independence from it. *Independence* here means that the human perception of well-being and selfhood is not dependent on external conditions. The confidence in the presence or awareness of self is impregnable to both material and social threats. Freedom is thus having attained a state of cognition (awareness) whereby persons perceive themselves as more than their roles and, in seeing this, are free to make society a reflection rather than a determinant of human potential.

I will conclude by saying that sociology's essential insight is, first, into the social nature of self-construction as an adaptive feature of the human organism. Through the processes of mind and society emerges the individual, the personality. Sociology's second and even greater insight is the significance of human consciousness in realizing that human subjectivity is unavailable in the social awareness of the self.

Sociology doesn't interpret reality; it shows us that the interpretations are a reality. What then comes into view is the reality of the ground of our social being. In this act, self-preservation has become the preservation of selflessness. The task is to practice maintaining this perception. By seeing social structure (sociology's provision of an essential insight), we learn that humans operate on a regular basis in the name of social self-interest. Then as easily as the law of aerodynamics kicks in when the air pressure under the wing of the aircraft is greater than above it and the 10-ton hunk of steel lifts, like a feather off the ground, we unsee social structure. We shift into the principle of another self-awareness or orientation, and we lift, like a feather, into a new realm of experience where only the laws of flight apply.

I frequent a Korean market on my way to the swimming pool to get some fruit and vegetables for quick energy. The cashier has difficulty speaking and understanding English, and customers are abrasive with her and she with them. They rumor that she is crooked and will try to "take you" on the cash register if you don't watch her. When I'm not worried about what she is going to do to me, I act differently than most people. At first, she was abrasive with me, too, only I never paid it any mind; I didn't emotionally lose myself because my self is founded beyond society. I asked her if Cindy was her real name and what her Korean name might be. She said, "Unmi." I repeated it and continued to refer to her by her Korean name when I would see her. I would always call her by name to ask for the lavender pen that was kept at the counter so that I could write my personal check to the store. I would also always remark about how nice I thought the lavender color was. Then, one day, when I went to ask Unmi for the pen, she handed me a gift box and said, "Open it." I did, and in it was a lavender pen. Without expecting, love reflects itself. Without striking out at Unmi like most customers, I had no judgment, no self-interest because she could do nothing to harm my real self. She changed her behavior, not because I told her to be good but because I let go of my self-interested perception of her.

Let's return to my reference about addiction: If we are defending what society says we deserve, then we are focused on the next "fix" and are never disinterested long enough to enjoy what self-giving will bring by virtue of its own principle.

GLOSSARY

I Self-awareness devoid of social self-awareness.

me Social self-awareness, the ego, personality; the familiar and seemingly natural way in which we come to be aware of ourselves as our social roles (male/female, Black/White, etc.).

preserving selflessness A mode of self-awareness or being oriented to expressing, serving, being disinterested in itself; self-preservation via giving up concern for self.

self-preservation A mode of self-awareness that is oriented toward self-defense.

society as object Society and the social role, or personality, are perceived as a self-realization independent of fundamental self-awareness.

society as subject A primitive form of consciousness in which the individual perceives himself only as society, *as* his social role rather than as expressing *through* it.

transcendence The experience of the self as more than a social self.

NOTES

1. George Herbert Mead, *Mind, Self and Society* (Chicago: University of Chicago Press, 1934).
2. See Mead.
3. Josiah Royce, *The Problem with Christianity: The Real World and the Christian Ideas*, vols. 1 and 2 (New York: Henry Regnery, 1971).
4. Joseph Campbell, "The Tiger and the Goat," in *The Hero's Journey: Joseph Campbell on His Life and Work*, ed. P. Cousineau (New York: Harper, 1990).
5. D. Lee, "Lineal and Nonlineal Codifications of Reality," *Psychosomatic Medicine*, 12 (May 1950): 89–97.
6. Maurice Merleau-Ponty, in *The Primacy of Perception*, ed. James M. Edie (Chicago: Northwestern University Press, 1964), p. 21. Merleau-Ponty declares that the certitude of existence is limited to pure and naked thought. As soon as thought is specific, we fail and have lost the "first truth." Social role, in other words, is not the first truth of existence.
7. *New York Times*, 21 May 1993, page C25.
8. See Merleau-Ponty.

10 SOCIOLOGY
Ageless and Always New

♦ EVOLUTION OF COOPERATION
AS EVOLUTION OF INDIVIDUAL CONSCIOUSNESS

We're Always Okay: It's Easy Once You Know the Way

Flashdance: "Feels Believin'"

♦ THE ROLE OF SOCIOLOGY IN THE UNDERSTANDING
AND STRUGGLE OF BECOMING HUMAN

A Metatheoretical Model of Social Determinism and Individual
Freedom: A Revival of Hegel's Consciousness Continuum and
Teilhard de Chardin's "Amorizing" of Hegel's Absolute Reason

Redefining the Limits of a Field of Study:
Departure from Ego Sociology

*I*f space and time permitted, I would introduce to you many others
who all are also society. So meet Everybody—those who shared
them-"selves" and everybody in general. We are not who you might
think we are, and, more importantly, we are not who we think we
are. We are not individuals as much as we are society.

To understand who we are, I again repeat that we must know
something about society, or the other humans with whom we live.
Fundamentally, we are amorphous protoplasm. Society embodies
itself as our personality—the consolidation of the group's instructions
about how we should feel and act toward things and others in the
world. Once we are able to see society as us, then what comes to
view is another level of self-perception and what it means to be an
individual. We unsee society by fixing our vision, or self-perception,
beyond society. In a way, we are not undoing what we have seen
but, by seeing anew, we are living by new principles. If we shift the
power of the lens, as on a microscope, we unsee what we just viewed
by taking on a different and new level of vision.

Meet Scot. He shares society as him. The principle of stratification is reflected in his self-judgment based on school achievement.

In September 1988, I enrolled in Fordham University, located in the Bronx, New York. By June 1991, I had failed out of a school I had come to deeply love, and I have been trying to recover ever since.[1]

Meet Sheila. She shares society as her. The principle of stratification is reflected in her self-judgment based on sexual standards for males and females.

In 1984, at the age of 11 years old, I was sexually abused; what effect will childhood sexual abuse have on me? Are the effects permanent?[2]

Meet Tami. She shares society as her. The principle of organization is reflected in her self-judgment based on standards for how much of our emotions and behaviors to share with persons. Society tells us how to respond to persons we are told to love. The mother-child bond is a particularistic relationship, defined by us sharing only with this person a wide array of sentiment and behavior. The loss of the mother can be the loss of oneself. The grief is the occasion for losing oneself or losing the grief by seeing social structure—by seeing that, even when we lose those we love, we do not lose ourselves.

About a year and a half ago, my mother passed away. She was very ill with lung cancer for a long time. When my mother finally passed away, my father and I fell into a deep depression.[3]

Meet Michelle. She shares society as her. As with Tami, the principle of organization is reflected in Michelle's self-judgment based on standards for how much of our emotions and behaviors to share with other people. Society tells us whom to love and how and for what reasons. When we violate society's instructions, we violate ourselves, but only then do we see social structure and conform or not conform, based on a new judgment of what it is to be a self.

Way back in the year 1947, my parents met for the first time. My father was the third son of two immigrant Italians who came straight off the boat and landed on Ellis Island. My mother was the fourth child out of ten. Her parents were Puerto Rican, and they, too, were immigrants whose destination was America. Each side of the family expected them to marry someone of their own back-

ground. I feel looked down upon because I am now involved in an interracial relationship.[4]

I could go on with more testimony of society as personality—as Vinnie, Rossan, Craig, Susan, Meryl, Tely, Joanna, and more. It doesn't matter whether it's cohabitation, homosexuality, ethnicity, or religion. When we come to know society—in all of its forms of cooperation and relatedness—we come to know ourselves. The better we are at feeling and acting toward others and things in the way society designates—whether as deviants or conformists—the more we feel like selves. But in seeing this, the forms have a new significance for us and for society. They are not us in the way we have come to know ourselves.

*A*t the gym where I practice the principles governing my physical body, I sweat and the muscles develop and conform to the image of their predisposition. Sociology is the same kind of realization—a set of principles—which, when observed and practiced, results in our conformity to a new image, one that has always been us as predisposition. The experience of individuality is actively and consciously called forth in the same way that the discipline of exercise brings bodily maturity.

Sociology is an understanding, and this understanding is the call for a new discipline of ourselves so that we can move on, developmentally, to what we are. It is a conscious, deliberate act of recognizing our ego's voice as an old thought form and the occasion for relying on the new one. We trust past diapers, pacifiers, and the breast and take on toilets, real food, and, more importantly, the stable consciousness that we need not seek food but identify with the properties of being that help us to find it. Sociology is ageless. It is premised on something that never changes, yet it is always new because it interprets the infinite number of social forms—our social positions, such as student, sibling, and the like—mechanisms for realizing and expressing that which is ageless. We see these structures, eventually, for the radiance of being, not for the acquisition of it.

EVOLUTION OF COOPERATION AS EVOLUTION OF INDIVIDUAL CONSCIOUSNESS

The tribute to sociology is for its two essential insights: seeing and unseeing social structure. Its talk is itself a social activity, an expression, an achievement of that which makes achievement possible to begin with. This work, as a social achievement, then, is that of setting forth new values as directives for our behavior. Itself a social activity (as the principles of socialization, organization, and so on), sociology accomplishes a means for seeing and understanding ourselves as creatures of cooperation. The cooperation is attained by a body of rules that regulate the self-interests of individual members in such a way that self-interest evolves in its appearance from a *getting* orientation to a *giving* orientation. To imagine in the sociological sense means seeing the obvious and beyond it. So, imagine that the final form of human evolutionary adaptation is its capacity for having by *giving* rather than having by *getting*. Don't worry that we won't have; it's the worrying that creates our personal and societal problems.

In more sophisticated language, the central contribution of sociological thought as an analytical tool for understanding why people behave the way they do lies in its distinctive shift in emphasis from individual to group determinants of behavior. This significance, however, is grossly understated because of confusion in the discipline over how to articulate the essential elements of its discourse. For example, one prominent delineation of sociology as a field of study is of the dialectical association between the individual and society on a continuum of social thought (from generality to specificity), so that the subject, or individual, ranges from being fully determined in her behavior to fully determining her behavior.

The consequence of this type of specification of the field is debate over what is uniquely the subject matter of sociology. This book has proposed a reformulation of the significance of sociology by introducing an integrated paradigm that, for its exemplar, revives the Hegelian (philosophical) formulation of social thought as subjective and objective properties of consciousness. The respecification of what is fundamentally sociological:

1. Isolates essential elements, social principles (universal laws), as a classification scheme for sociological phenomena and shows how theories explain the nature of these principles and
2. Demonstrates that the domain of individual freedom is found outside the discourse of science as a residual category, and the role of sociology, as a form of consciousness, is developmental, a precondition for realizing human subjectivity. Reciprocally, consequences of the realization of individual freedom are for society and social structure.

We're Always Okay: It's Easy Once You Know the Way

Ironically, my obsession with sociology has been about not having to be obsessed about anything. I think sociology is so wonderful because I claim it understands our behavior and, as an understanding, fosters human development. Sociology, in its essential insights, shifts our focus, which allows us to unsee what we have seen about ourselves at the social level of being human. Sociology doesn't talk as much about specific needs or desires—how to be rich and famous, how to get good grades, how to have big breasts, how to be loving if our parents didn't love us the right way—as much as it talks about a new way of talking about these very things. Sociology says that, hypothetically, couples in the United States might fall in love because they have eyelashes of the same length, not because of some mathematical attraction or some other great and profound mystery but simply because of the alignment of society's instructions as individual personality. Sociology also says that, according to society's standards, when Adam doesn't want to marry, he is not wise, naive, or mentally unstable but deviant because his rules for relating to others vary from what the group values.

Then sociology tells us that, in the inevitable process of our becoming human by becoming selves according to what is important for the group or society, a number of consequences can happen: poor self-esteem, depression, alcoholism, and group superiority. These negative outcomes do not come from Long Beach or from too much fluoridation in our drinking water; they come from our *becoming* our roles as opposed to *expressing* ourselves through our roles. It's strange how things move without effort once we see our attachment and rest in the completeness of our being before imposing on it social standards for worth. Once we know the way, that we're first and always the self we try to achieve, we have realized that new place in our self-perception. It's easy.

Flashdance: "Feels Believin'"

Freedom from social determinism—for instance, feeling miserable because you have small breasts—does not mean changing the situation by getting falsies or implants, by starting a protest against advocates of big breasts, or by associating with other females who have small breasts. All of these responses presume that big breasts define women's humanness, and as long as that's the case, we will try, one way or another, to defend the definition. The problem becomes transformed into the occasion for asking if all there is to being human is one definition or another. And, of course, sociology's retort is No!

The change in the situation is through the realization that self-worth is not based on breast size. In the movie *Flashdance*, a young female nightclub dancer who worries about whether she can *do* ballet realizes she just has to *be* it. She changes from feeling that it just can't happen to feeling "believin'."

▲ THE ROLE OF SOCIOLOGY IN THE UNDERSTANDING AND STRUGGLE OF BECOMING HUMAN

In sum, sociology says we're not who we think we are and then asks us to consider, Who are we? It changes our self-perception from one of *doing* to one of *being*. We are able to see by unseeing. Our being accepts rather than achieves our part for us. Everything we do is not by personal proprietorship but under a new auspices, where everything social is the avenue and the extension of the most basic self. This self does not agonize or struggle to maintain itself, as does the social self. It concerns itself not with what it wants to do but with realizing who it is and in finding that it does what it has to better. It identifies not the answers to its questions but the source that makes it question at all.

Sociology's essential insights of seeing and unseeing represent a shift in our sense of purpose. Usually, we are driven to search for our self, to defend it, or to give it up but to change our attachments to these ideas of self. These modes of talk, or discourse, pertain to who we think we are before we find a new sense of identity. We lose our preoccupation with who we thought we were and, in so doing, automatically become what we thought we had to be.

Sociology expands our ability to realize fully what we are. Sociology reveals that our sense of feeling better or worse than others is illusory and breeds fear and self-defense. Sociology restores to us the recognition of what we are without having to achieve it. Our social selves tell us that we're not enough just by being. Selflessness is a state of experience where the self is devoid of any thought, conscious or unconscious, of itself. This does not mean nonself, or the doing away with the self; rather, it means doing away with the thought of the self. The unthinking self is one *as it is in itself* versus one as *it is known to itself.* It is a state of awareness unconditioned by the laws of thought—the thing-in-itself, a Kantian "ding-an-sich."[5]

Sociology knows that we have been temporarily unaware; our humanhood is in us, not of us. My friend's six-year-old niece, when asked what she is going to be when she grows up, said, "Be? I *am*." Being a genius or an idiot is okay by a new standard of judgment, the occasion for the expression of giving, not being reduced to one or the other. Forgetting this causes fear and loss of trust in our fundamental strength; at this level of self-awareness, we will be fretful.

A Metatheoretical Model of Social Determinism and Individual Freedom: A Revival of Hegel's Consciousness Continuum and Teilhard de Chardin's "Amorizing" of Hegel's Absolute Reason

Here is a very technical rendition of what is, in plain talk, sociology's contributions.

What Georg Hegel[6] really saw was that sociology doesn't talk about reality but is a reality, a level of awareness of the world. Pierre Teilhard de Chardin[7] "amorized" the term and saw the grounds on which reason is possible at all. The *divine milieu* is reason by grace or love—reason in the service of others. Sociological awareness is a step in the evolution of society by means of the evolution of the individual's awareness of herself in relation to society.

Redefining the Limits of a Field of Study: Departure from Ego Sociology

The remarkable things about sociology have been missed. Yes, for most people, the world is flat, but for one, it is round. Mistakenly, conventional renderings of sociology have focused on the social self, but this discussion has been a departure from such ego sociologies. Extant sociologies have not been able to talk adequately about what is individual about us, to find just what constitutes freedom for a social creature. The reexamination of sociology is actually part of the development of individual freedom because it is able to show us what is social about us and what else makes being social possible. Sociology provides for the realization that we are not society after all, and when we don't think we need society to be ourselves, we are ourselves. The understanding and practice of sociology's essential insights makes available the restoration of individual awareness and the possibility of a society that reflects cooperation as provisions for giving rather than for a lawful regulation of self-interest.

The final word about sociology is that it must be clear about the subject matter of its study and it must be reflexive by recognizing that the study itself is a level of development in human consciousness. The first role of sociology is the scientific study of the social realm. Sociology is a peculiar degree of actuality,[8] a property of consciousness, a scientific perception of what is real. As a science, it is neatly specified as the relation of principles of social life to the theories explaining them. The many sociologies are encompassed under the rubric of principles and accompanying theories.

The second role of sociology is as an idea, an awareness, that acts as a stepping stone in the individual's development. Sociology, as a property of consciousness, is a precondition for freedom. The individual's social self-awareness (a fundamental prerequisite for cooperation) is grounded in the larger context of prereflective awareness through the process of disidentification. The prereflective state of awareness is restored; social roles thus become the opportunity for expression of a self not governed by social self-defense. The disinterested self has consequences for the emergence of the ideal society, the loving community.

The dual contributions of sociology have been introduced in a model (derived from the presuppositions of Hegelian philosophy) of social determinism and individual freedom as three properties of subjective and objective consciousness: *prereflective, social scientific,* and *transcendent* (see Figure 10.1).[9] The ability to talk adequately about the dialectic relationship of the individual and society is contingent on identifying the realm of individual freedom as outside the domain of scien-

FIGURE 10.1

A metatheoretical model of social determinism (collective order) and individual freedom (voluntary action)

Prereflective	Social Scientific	Transcendent
	Theories[b] Principles/Laws	
	—Organization	
	—Stratification	
	—Social control/deviance	
	—Social change	
	—Socialization	
	—Institutions	

(Instrumental/Rational/Self-preserving orientation to order and action)   *(Self-giving orientation to order and action)*

———▶

c ◀———————————

Properties of Subjective and Objective Consciousness[a]

Note: *See note 9, pages 128–129, for explanations of lettered notes in this figure.*

Source: *From* Sociology of Education: Theoretical and Empirical Investigations, *by Lynn M. Mulkey, copyright © 1993 by Holt, Rinehart and Winston, Inc., reprinted by permission of the publisher.*

tific discourse. The individual is first and always social; the recognition of social identity is the very precursor of individual freedom. One must be constrained to be free. Freedom then results in conformity or nonconformity on the basis of the new standard of self-giving.[10]

By redefining the limits of sociology as a field of study (a reality) in terms of three properties of consciousness, this "introduction to introductions to sociology" represents a departure from ego sociology. That departure is in respecifying the role of sociology as both the understanding and the struggle of becoming human. The metatheoretical model of social determinism and individual freedom, based on a revival of Hegel's consciousness continuum, introduces and underscores the paradoxical notion that sociology is less the study of *groups* and more the study of *individuals*. Ultimately, sociological understanding results in the achievement, the realization of what it means to be an individual. Paradoxically, for sociology to be the epitome of science—*seeing* to believe—it must integrate into its understanding the notion of *unseeing*, an awareness of the thing seeing to believe.

GLOSSARY

ego sociology   Sociology that emphasizes social determinism; study of the group and the influence that it has on individual behavior with a focus on less rather than more voluntary action on the part of the individual.

metatheoretical model of social determinism   The integration of all social theories as explanations of the principles of sociology.

prereflective self   Self-awareness prior to the imposition of social role.

role of sociology   The dual insights of (1) a scientific understanding of the relationship of the individual to the group (others) and (2) the consequences of this understanding for the development of human freedom and what it means to be an individual in the group.

NOTES

1. Reprinted with permission of the author.
2. Reprinted with permission of the author.
3. Reprinted with permission of the author.
4. Reprinted with permission of the author.
5. For more discussion, see Mihaly Csikszentmihalyi, *Flow: The Psychology of Optimal Experience* (New York: Harper Collins, 1990), and Benito Reyes, *Moments without Self* (Philippines: M. Colid, 1970).
6. Georg W. F. Hegel, *The Phenomenology of Mind* (New York: Harper Colophon, 1967; originally printed in 1807).

7. Pierre Teilhard de Chardin, *The Divine Milieu: An Essay on the Interior Life* (New York: Harper & Row, 1960).
8. Nickolai Berdyaev, *Slavery and Freedom* (New York: Charles Scribner's Sons, 1944).
9. Notes to Figure 10.1 (quoted from Lynn M. Mulkey, *Sociology of Education: Theoretical and Empirical Investigations* [Orlando, FL: Harcourt Brace Jovanovich, 1993], pp. xvi–xvii):

"*Consciousness is used here to denote various states of awareness (what the individual perceives as real or a reality). Mind, an instrument of sensation (visual, auditory, tactile, olfactory, and gustatory), emotion, volition, and thought* transmits awareness *via the brain. Inherent in the cognitive domain of consciousness is the capacity for memory and a social predisposition, that is, the capacity to acquire language and to cooperate through rule-making and rule-following activity. (Neurophenomenology, for example, endeavors to explain the predisposition or innate structural antecedents to cooperate as essences, basic forms of cooperation devoid of cultural conditioning, by reference to invariant neurognostic structures which constrain both cognitions and perceptions—see Warren TenHouten's "Into the Wild Blue Yonder: On the Emergence of the Ethnoneurologies, the Social Sci-ence- and Philosophy-Based Neurosciences,"* Journal of Social and Biological Structures, *1991, 14:381–408.) The manifestation of these inherent and invari-ant structures is indicated in the figure as* principles and laws. *Principles refer to the law-like, cooperative, rule-making and rule-following predisposition of individ-uals that, when objectified in collective form, appear as types of behavioral pre-scriptions (social structure; society). The principles comprise a level of scientific precision or determinateness; they appear universally in all human groups as cate-gories of behavioral directives. These essential elements of social life are the social structural determinants of consciousness and the social self (personality). Simulta-neously, social self consciousness is externalized in collective form and objectified as society. Society is cause, the individual the effect; society is a macro-determi-nant of human behavior; the social self is in the world and "of it." Society is order and determinism, law, morality, and the regulation of self-interest. Society affirms rather than confirms Self. Theories explain the nature of the operation or dynam-ics of principles.* Consciousness, *also as it is referred to here, also includes the direct awareness of* Self. *The individual is able to* transcend *the social self (aban-don all mental and internalized conceptions of self) and experience (realize) a pre-reflective state of awareness of Self—the Self, alienated in the consciousness of the individual in the formative process of social self-objectification. (See Maurice Merleau-Ponty's* The Phenomenology of Perception, *translated by Colin Smith, London: Routledge & Kegan Paul, 1962. Like J. P. Sartre, he viewed freedom as the capacity of consciousness to transcend its "situation," to another level of aware-ness. Also see Peter Berger's "Religion and World Construction," in* The Sacred Canopy: Elements of a Sociology Theory of Religion, *New York: Doubleday, 1967, and Morris Rosenberg's "Self-Objectification: Relevance for the Species and Society," in* Sociological Forum *3: 548–565, 1988.) The significance of acknowl-edging, after socialization, the Self that exists antecedent to the social self is for the subject's freedom from social determinism. The subject is thus "in society, but not of it" in that she or he is free to "express" Self through social structure rather than "equate" Self with it. The transcendent property of consciousness represents the evolution of cooperation as the evolution of individual consciousness. It refers to a process of realization as opposed to an investigation, a search for self through cognitive activity of the mind. At this level, society is the object and the individual the subject, and social change results less from changing social structure and more from changes in one's view of it. At this phase in the developmental continuum of consciousness, G. W. F. Hegel's characterization of consciousness as "absolute reason" is more accurately typified by Thomas Aquinas's (1985) habit of equating love with Being or Teilhard de Chardin's (1960, 1964) "amorization" of absolute reason. In other words, love is simply a disinterested reason, or reason stripped of self-interest. The shift in consciousness marks a departure from ego sociology and the finding of oneself "in the normal distribution." Here, sociology means the breaking down of social-self defense, a "sociotherapy" of exercises in desocialization, a transformation that results in the individual's being in society, but not of it. Consequences of the transcendent orientation to cooperation are for individual psychological well-being and for the actualization of the ideal community (representations of levels of consciousness are found in societal forms such as communism, socialism, democracy, and so on). In this state of Self-awareness, the subject is free from, or impervious to, material and social threats to its annihilation. At this stage on the continuum of awareness, thought is non-recursive, nonlinear, and acts back on society with consequences for social structure.*

[b]*See George Ritzer's* Sociological Theory, *New York: Knopf, 1988, as an exemplary documentation of the many explanations of social principles. Functional, conflict, symbolic interactionist, and others are the typical fare or jargon.*

[c]*The vector pointing left indicates that "transcending" society has consequences for society. Mainly, when persons realize the "prereflective" Self, social structure represents the relations of a "loving" community espoused by Josiah Royce in* The Problem of Christianity, Vol. II: The Real World and the Christian Ideas, *Chicago: Henry Regney, 1968, in contrast to the law as an external regulation of self-interest.*

10. Quoted from Mulkey, p. 252, note 2:

Varied ideas of an evolution of individual consciousness are found in the works of G. F. W. Hegel, "Introduction," in The Philosophy of History *(Carl J. Friedrich, ed., New York: The Modern Library, 1954) and Pierre Teilhard de Chardin,* The Future of Man. *For Hegel, the history of humankind is the history of the gradual unfolding of the Spirit; this is a history marked by stages in which the Absolute Spirit evolves into its own. Humans slowly arrive at true self-consciousness. Teilhard de Chardin similarly posits a historical evolution of consciousness. These conceptions of progress focus on growth in society as a whole, and de-emphasize the significance that an individual can have in changing the course of history by moving from the level of law and morality to the level of love and freedom.*

INDEX

Note: Bold page numbers indicate definitions in chapter-ending glossaries.

ABOUT THE AUTHOR

Lynn M. Mulkey earned a Ph.D. in 1985 from Columbia University with a specialization in the sociology of education. This specialization emerged from studies with Bernard Barber in the sociology of knowledge, with R. K. Merton and Harriet Zuckerman in the sociology of scientific knowledge, and with Sloan R. Wayland in the sociology of knowledge and education.

Although Dr. Mulkey has been exposed to the gamut of sociological theoretical formulations and their accompanying methodologies, she has been most influenced by Emile Durkheim, Talcott Parsons, and R. K. Merton in the tradition of functionalist theory; by Peter Berger in humanistic theory; and by Harold Garfinkel in ethnomethodology. She is practiced in a number of modes of observation (survey, evaluation, experiment, field, and content analysis) and has special expertise in evaluation research.

Dr. Mulkey was recently a National Institute of Mental Health Fellow and Visiting Assistant Professor in the Department of Sociology at the University of California, Los Angeles, and has a regular appointment as an Assistant Professor of Sociology at Hofstra University. She enjoys teaching both undergraduate and graduate students and has taught classes in introductory sociology, research methods, sociology of education, social psychology, and contemporary sociological theory, among others.

Dr. Mulkey is also employed as an evaluation research consultant by the New York City Board of Education Office of Research, Evaluation, and Assessment, where she supervises and conducts large-scale federally, state-, and locally mandated and funded assessments (e.g., Chapter I) of the effectiveness of educational programs implemented in the city's public schools. She has authored numerous journal articles and research reports and likes to talk about the utility of sociology for enriching the human experience through its understanding.